CMF SURVIVAL MANUAL

CMF SURVIVAL MANUAL

Disaster Response & Survival Field Guide

Authored by usCrow.org - SSG R. M. Lanesra

For those we never let go,
But have to leave behind...

"Democracy will soon degenerate into an anarchy, such an anarchy that every man will do what is right in his own eyes and no man's life or property or reputation or liberty will be secure, and every one of these will soon mould itself into a system of subordination of all the moral virtues and intellectual abilities, all the powers of wealth, beauty, wit and science, to the wanton pleasures, the capricious will, and the execrable cruelty of one or a very few." -John Adams

TABLE OF CONTENTS

Bush Survival

Cheat Sheets

GENERAL

INTRODUCTION

From the outside looking in prepping could easily be intimidating to individuals or families who are unfamiliar with the practice. Most unfamiliar things are. When considering you and your family's commitment to prepping and survival, you should consider if you have a genuine and rational threat you are preparing for. Most of the survival community accepts disaster can strike at any time, and anywhere. It's not surprising the majority of survival communities are families. At its core it is a genetic response to protect your family when triggered by your level of awareness to a potential threat. In short, it is human nature to prepare and survive. So there is no need for anyone to feel indifferent. So let's jump in, here's the basics for Prepping and Survival.

Reasons to be Prepping

The question you should ask yourself is what is logical and the most likely SHTF Scenario *(Shit Hits the Fan)* Scenario. Are you concerned about a catastrophic man-made or natural disaster that will devastate the global populace or your country, or are you more concerned with a localized event such as; tidal wave, tornado, flooding & etc.? Asking yourself this will assist you in targeting your specific needs. Another common household reason for prepping is an international economic collapse, which is a logical concern. Besides, FEMA advises that at a minimum, all Americans should have a three-day disaster back-up plan.

Bugging In or Bugging Out

Evaluate your threat and make a determination if it requires you to bug out from your current location to a more rural and less populated area. In almost any instance when you are located in a heavily populated metropolitan area a bug out will be required. Let's face it, when SHTF the masses do not play well with one another. In more rural areas it is more likely you will want to bunker down. However, you have to evaluate your situation. If you are located below sea level and in a rural area you will need to bug out to a secondary location at higher elevation.

In short, practice common sense and deductive logic when making your determinations. When a Bug Out is required will you need a Bug Out Bag BOB for each one of your family members for extended travel. Bunkering Down in a shelter requires food stockpiling, water stockpiling. You can start with the 23 basic and critical items for food storage, as an introductory list of inexpensive staples to add to your pantry.

How much food should you store?

First you will need to determine how long you and your family will have to live without a grocery store in your SHTF scenario. In any disaster in the past, it was the grocery stores' shelves to be emptied in as little as 24 hours. Mass hysteria is also human nature when disaster strikes. When making your assessment simply understand a minimum of 1,500 calories are required to prevent malnutrition a day, while 2,000 calories is a more comfortable daily intake. Multiplying the amount of people in your group by 2,000 calories for each day will provide you the required daily caloric consumption. Now you can determine the amount of food you will need based on your situation. If order is not restored in your SHTF Scenario you should store food and invest in sustainable food sources such as hunting, fishing and farming.

Protection and Defense

If this is not your first time to usCrow you'll notice we focus on personal defense, which is required for any disaster. If you're a realist you'd understand America has a lot of jails and prisons for a reason, because people to bad things. There will always be evil in the world, without a basic policing force things can go bad quickly. So what exactly can you do to defend you and your family? First, take instructional and firearms safety classes if you're not familiar with firearms. Purchase a firearm before Obama the Communist uses executive orders to ban them. Then, determine the force and ability required for threats. At a bare minimum you could easily use Hurricane Sandy as an example where gun-owners were required to defend their property.

Basic Hygiene and First Aid

It's possible you won't have a hospital or an ER to go to when SHTF, while hygiene is often neglected in most bunker down repertories. So when storing don't forget the TP, toothpaste, detergents and etc. Educate yourself and your family members in Basic First Aid and Trauma Response. First Aid Kits and Supplies should be a part of your BOB, Bunker, and Vehicles. When we're downrange or out in the field we bring a USMC Individual First Aid Kit IFAK with us which are lightweight and easy to transport.

Power Failure when SHTF

Power grids go out all the time, look at any natural disaster since electricity was implemented into everyday life. Now your air conditioning relies on that same power grid, which includes your lighting. Such a rapid loss of these essentials can be traumatic on morale when you're in darkness fourteen hours out of the day. So prepare by stocking up on batteries, fuel, and alternative energy such as firewood to heat your home, solar cells, gas generators, wind and etc. Again, determine the threat and assess the time you will be required to live off grid. When you make this assertion try to overshoot the estimate for good measure. You can see the typical pricing in our Prepper and Bunker Surplus for alternative energy sources.

Dehydration; the not-so-silent killer.

Every day you lose water through your breath, perspiration, urine and bowel movements. For your body to function properly, you must replenish its water supply. So how much fluid does the average, healthy adult living in a temperate climate need? The Institute of Medicine determined that an adequate intake (AI) for men is roughly 3 liters (about 13 cups) of total beverages a day. The AI for women is 2.2 liters (about 9 cups) of total beverages a day. You should always have a back-up supply of water regardless of your beliefs. However use this example to adequately stockpile water, if it is a perpetual lack of fresh water look into filtration systems and etc.

Prepper Funding

Prepping can and will cost you some money based on your individual level of involvement. A good practice to adhere with a reasonable timeline of a two-year minimum before SHTF would allow you to commit 10% of your income to savings, precious metals, diversified portfolios and etc. while allowing 5% of your income to be spent on your prepping. If you're in a more rural area with an abundance of natural vegetation prepping food could cost you relatively less if you invest in private farming, where not much acreage is required if you're preserving and dehydrating your crops. There are an abundance of guides to bush crafting and living off the land in the usCrow Field Guides and Manuals. Another thing to consider is what you could barter after SHTF such as alcohol, precious metals, and other goods the less fortunate will want to trade for.

REASONS TO PREPARE

Believe it or not we use to have a common thread between us that understood disasters are inevitable. The usCrow 'Top 5 Reasons to be a Prepper' are incredibly more common and unending than you may realize.

Should you be a prepper?

Across the U.S., Americans have let their guards down, committing their absolute faith and confidence in the federal government's bureaucracies that continue to drop the ball. When time and history continue to prove deniers wrong the question has to be asked, why are you not preparing for at least one of these Top 5 Reasons to be a Prepper? Think it out and understand it doesn't take anything more than responsibility and education to prepare for SHTF (Shit to Hit the Fan).

5. Viral Pandemic

We have a reasonable amount of faith in our medical professionals and the CDC (Centers for Disease Control), but we're still forced to accept that a mutated strain of Ebola can spread across our globe in as little as a few weeks. From 1976 to 2011 there have been 28 known cases of Ebola (Hemorrhagic Fever) outbreaks, and three of those outbreaks were in the United States of America. There is no known cure for Ebola, and when an artificial or natural mutation occurs in its strain our country will be absolutely defenseless. Pandemics like Ebola are devastating to any population regardless of their scientific advancements. For instance, the most devastating pandemic known as 'The Black Death' occurred in the fourteenth century. In as little as two years The Black Death mortality rate quickly rose to approximately two hundred million fatalities. However, these cases lacked modern medicine and 'over-night' international travel.

Worried yet? Well, there's a reason Viral Pandemic is only listed as Number 5 on our Reasons to be a Prepper. America leads the way in microbiology and medical advancements, including several other countries throughout the globe who don't want the entire species to go extinct. In addition to the natural outbreak of a population leveling virus, you also have to prepare for an intentional release by man. Humans have a history of being self-destructive and unbalanced when fueled by some insane ideology, being a prepper could save your and your family's life.

4. Cyber Attack

The digital infrastructure of The United States is the internet, and it's not adequately protected as seen in the latest rise of publicized cyber-attacks on American interests. If our digital infrastructure does not undergo immediate advancements in defense technology the attacks will only become more frequent and more damaging. Think about it, no more money from the ATM because the world's banking systems have been successfully hacked. Without money to exchange hands our economy would collapse, causing the remaining countries' economies follow in America's steps due to international banking and trading reliance, and vice versa.

The most prominent case of cyber-attacks against American Institutions occurred between October 2011 and February 2012, with 50,000 successful attacks reported to the Department of Homeland Security and 86 of attacks on critical infrastructure networks. Critical infrastructure networks such as; power grid, basic communication (cell phones, broadcasts, and internet access), water supplies, oil production and delivery, agriculture (no more food from the store).

When you think about it, we continue to produce synthetic processing power advancements, making processors faster and smarter, which follow a trending escalation in the severe complexity of cyber-attacks. Common sense should tell you cyber-attack is a potential threat to you, your family and friends.

3. Economic Collapse

According to the Bureau of Labor Statistics the U.S. Labor Force percentage of employed Americans has continued to decline since 2006. You will hear magical platitudes about these numbers, but the realities are plain as beans at times. The increase of Americans that are no longer in the labor force since Obama was elected in 2008 is no more than three times greater than the increase in the rates of the 1980's. With governments across the globe invading the private sector it's no surprise liquid and independent capitalism is crippled.

A devastating -.01 GDP (Gross Domestic Product) announced in January 2013 followed a continuous pattern of economic recession since 2008. According to the USDA the number of Americans who rely upon the government for basic needs has reached a record high of 47,710,324+/- or 15%. All the numbers are pointing towards economic collapse, the middle class will inevitably be taxed at a pervasive level and our Country's economy will be finished. What's Obama's answer after spending six trillion dollars in four years with only negative and downward sloping results? Tax more Americans and spend more, that's called the brass tacks. This makes economic collapse a valid reason to be a prepper.

2. Natural Disaster

Natural disasters are common in America, tornadoes occur at least a thousand times every year, 12% of the population was threatened by a hurricane in 2011, mega floods occur every 100-200 years and since 1980 there has been over 410 recorded droughts. With high probability stats like these natural disasters takes a well-deserved 2nd place reason to be a prepper. Natural disasters are common enough and relatively simple enough to prepare for. A lack of preparedness contributed to the death rates of Katrina, where approximately 971 deaths were due to drowning, murder, and etc...

A basic approach to prepping would have saved countless lives in Katrina and other natural disasters with a minimal amount of preparedness required. Natural disasters are not a threat to continental and global populations but they can still do a lot of damage based on their severity. Basic preparedness and basic knowledge saves lives. Always have a means of defense and survival for you and your family.

1. WAR

In 238 Years America has been in 17 major wars, and over 47 Attacks were on American Soil and Embassies since 1920... that we know about. Pax Romana was stable and prosperous for two hundred years before its first major crisis that was well survived. Now we have countries like North Korea quickly becoming a threat to the United States and our allies, they are firmly tied to China and their government is actively trying to invade Japanese lands to pillage their natural resources through slow, but continuous strikes.

We have stood with Israel since 1948 and they are at the brink of war with Egypt (The Muslim Brotherhood whose first bylaw is Jihad) and Iran (Ran by Muslim Extremists whose first bylaw is Jihad, and we're letting them build Nukes.), and now Barack Obama has approved sending several M1A1 Abrams Tanks and F16's to Egypt. Now factor in Russia, who will defend Bashir Assad's Syrian Regime and Iran if America takes action. Now you have a perfect set of circumstances for global war. This information is not being broadcasted in the main stream media and you will have to learn for yourself without being spoon fed what to believe.

So the Top Reason for you to be a Prepper or Survivalist is War, the most common disaster Americans face. Maybe having some supplies stored and firearms at the ready wouldn't be such a bad idea. Never forget, America has a wealth of resources and the rest of the world is quickly depleting their own, by then the laws of human nature are inescapable.

BASIC SURVIVAL SKILLS

There are 5 Basic Outdoor Survival Skills that everyone who ventures into the Outdoors should understand and be fully aware of their potential need and use. This is a just brief outline, not a full explanation of all the requirements and items required in each category. One of the most important elements to survival is between your ears, your brain. DO NOT PANIC, use your wits and practice all elements of the 5 Basics before you may need to rely on them.

Survival Skills - Fire

Fire can purify water, cook food, signal rescuers, provide warmth, light and comfort, help keep predators at a distance, and can be a most welcome friend and companion. Each and every person who ventures into the Outdoors should have a minimum of two ways to start a fire with them, one on their person at all times and the other with their gear. A few small fires provide more heat than one large fire. Collect firewood you think you will need for the night and then collect the same amount again, experience shows you will need it. Conserve fuel by making a "star fire" where the ends of large logs meet in the fire only, push inward as more fuel is needed. Make a reflector from your SPACE BLANKET on the back wall of a shelter to reflect heat of your survival fire to your back, sit between fire and back shelter wall.

Survival Skills - Shelter

Shelter is the means by which you protect your body from excess exposure from the sun, cold, wind, rain or snow. Anything that takes away or adds to your overall body temperature can be your enemy. Clothing is the first line of shelter protection, have the right clothes for the right environment. Always have a hat. Try and keep the layer closest to your body dry. Layers trap air and are warmer than one thick garment. Do not expend energy making a shelter if nature provides one. Practice building a quick *'lean-to shelter'* in case you cannot find your campsite, do not wait until you need to make one. Use a SPACE BLANKET to prevent dampness or to insulate your shelter or to wrap yourself up in a sitting or squat position to concentrate your body core heat.

Signaling

Signaling is having available the means and ability to alert any and all potential rescuers that you are in need of HELP. Fire, flashing light, bright color markers, flags, mirrors, whistles all will help you be found. Three fires in a triangular form are a recognized distress signal. Carefully bank your signal fires to prevent igniting surrounding area. Use regular signal mirrors only when you can see a plane, or people in the distance. Use emergency strobe lights at night to help attract attention from those that may be in the area. Make smoky fire with organic material over the fire during the day to attract attention. Lay out ground to air signal in open field, S.O.S. from rocks, logs or colored clothing, whatever will be seen against the background. Most search and rescue parties use aircraft as a primary method of sighting.

Food & Water

Food and Water are vital towards your survival. Ration your sweat not your water intake. Try to drink only in the cool of the evening. You can live up to three days without water. DO NOT eat plants you do not know. Never drink urine. Always assume that you will need extra food and water when you plan your trip. Pack energy bars and candy in your pockets at all time, just in case. If possible boil all water 10 minutes plus one minute for every 1000 feet above sea level. Strain water through your handkerchief to remove large particles. Try to drink only in the cool of the evening. Never wait until you are without water to collect it.

Have some poly zip bags to collect and store water. Never eat any wild berries that you are not sure of what they are. You can catch rain water in your space blanket by laying it out in a trench.

First Aid

First Aid is not just the basic medical needs; it is the primary way in which you act to survive. DO NOT PANIC, remain calm and do what you have to do to take care of yourself. STOP means Sit, Think, Observe, and Plan. It is the most intelligent thing you can do when you realize you are lost or stranded. The most important element is to keep your brain functioning rationally; this is basic first aid for survival.

USCROW

Analyze your needs before every trip; create a medical checklist and carry a small personal kit with you at all times. Most survival situations require only dressing for small cuts, bruises and personal medication needs, make sure you know what you have with you and how to use it. Do not over pack; pack what you feel you will need to carry with you at all times. Concentrate on being found, pack a picture of your family in with your gear to remind you of the reasons to remain calm and to survive. Prevent hypothermia by insulating yourself in a space blanket.

SURVIVAL KIT PREPARATION

An efficient B.O.B. ('Bug Out Bag') is a mobile cache of various items required for surviving short periods of time when Shit Hits The Fan. The BOB should be prepared in advance since you won't have the luxury of time to purchase or gather the supplies you need. Having an adequate and versatile Bug out Bag stocked and ready will increase your chances of survival during emergency evacuations.

Included below are notes to help you get started and an example of one individual's BOB All members of your family or group should have a BOB, tailored to their individual needs.

The survival kit in this example is adequate for this particular individual; make sure your individual needs are satisfied.

Survival Kit Key Notes

- *Make sure your BOB is located in a convenient and secure location.*
- *Alert family members (if applicable) to the location of their BOB's.*
- *Rotate stored food in your Bug out Bag*
- *Store medication and prescriptions in your BOB and rotate as needed.*
- *Survival requires First Aid/CPR Certification for you and your family.*
- *Continuously improve your Bug out Bag as your needs change.*

Recommended Bug Out Bag

Spec-Ops T.H.E. Pack – This product has been tested in the field by operators across the world, attesting to its quality. With features like these it's easy to understand why:

- *Cordura 1000D Nylon Fabric Durability*
- *#10 Zippers on Main Compartments and Outer Pockets*
- *Double Layer Pack Top Eliminating Stress Failures*
- *Dual Compression Straps with Load Loops*

- *Removable Waist Belt and Endless Adjustments*
- *MTX Harness Compatible*

Bug Out Bag – Water

Store water for your BOB's in sealed plastic containers to prevent contamination. Include a minimum of a three-day water supply or 2 quarts a day for each member of your family. Intense physical activities such as running or extreme stress will double the amount of water your body requires. If a Bug Out Vehicle is available and you must choose between water and food, choose water. For best results include the following items with your survival kit's water supplies:

- *Water bladder for convenience*
- *Flavoring pouches for variety*
- *Water filtration straws for backup water intake*
- *Water purification tablets for backup water intake*

Bug Out Bag – Food

Include at least a three-day food supply of non-perishable food in your Survival Kit. Dehydrated foods are absolutely essential for you BOB. Unlike canned foods, dehydrated food is freeze-dried, making it compact and light weight. It requires little water to make and takes up minimal space in your kit. Be sure to compensate for special dietary needs as required. In addition to dehydrated meals consider including:

- *High protein energy bars for physical activity*
- *C-Rations for emergency use*
- *Multivitamins to prevent malnutrition*
- *M.R.E.'s (Meals Ready to Eat)*

Bug Out Bag – First Aid and Medications

First aid kits and medical supplies should be fully stocked in all BOB's. Under-stocked First Aid Kits will cost lives in an emergency. However, medical first aid kits are practically useless if you don't have the training to properly use the supplies. Search locally to find affordable or free courses and certification classes.

- *Field use First Aid Kit*
- *Bug Out Bag First Aid Kit*

Medication should be well thought out in your survival kit based on your needs. For example; if you have a diabetic in your group or family you will want to include insulin pens, test strips, electric portable camping cooler, and adequate rotation procedures.

Bug Out Bag – Additional Supplies

- *Solar or crank powered flashlight*
- *Fire source*
- *Additional clothing*
- *Sanitation wipes*
- *Extra cash or bartering items*
- *Waterproof gear*
- *Personal identification*
- *Knife*
- *Multifunctional tool set*
- *USB Jump Drive for essential information*
- *Local maps*
- *Emergency blanket*
- *Para-cord*
- *Sunscreen repellent*
- *Single person tent*
- *Lighter fluid, oil*
- *Entertainment for children (if applicable)*

Again design your Bug out Bag to fit each individual's needs based on their size and circumstances. Paying attention to the fine details makes a successful kit.

Bug Out Bag – Weapons

In any emergency situation personal protection is an absolute requirement; we don't have prisons in America because society is full of angels. Rioting, looting, physical/sexual assault is common. Firearms, knives, hatchets, crossbows, non-lethal defense items such as a taser or baton, and even certain household objects will be vital to protecting you and your family members should the need arise. These tools should be properly maintained and readily available in your BOB. Most importantly, you and your family should be properly trained to use these weapons. Maintaining proficiency will help eliminate panic and greatly improve your chances of survival.

BASIC GOODS TO STORE

We reviewed 123survivalplan, a video that is supposed to provide the public with 37 critical food items that are considered *'must have'* for any prepper's doomsday and survival plan. However, it turned out to be a 10 minute long commercial to influence you to pay for it. Yes, we love capitalism but it doesn't bode well for our sense of patriotism to charge Americans for information about survival. So, in response we will provide our own list.

Before we hit the precipice of disaster any good prepper and survivalist should have a minimum of 6 months' worth of food *(usCrow has set the minimum lower due to recessive incomes).* Any given grocery or goods store has a maximum of 3 days' worth of goods to last if their supply chain is cut off in the event of a disaster, and that doesn't include the looting factor.

Grocery Stores are gone when the SHTF

There's nothing worse than facing a disaster, running to the grocery store to buy what you need to survive and finding out the shelves have been picked dry…and now your family is going to starve. At the very least, you should prepare for your family's sake. Keep in mind, water isn't listed but that item should be obvious. In addition, MRE's (Meals Ready to Eat) are specifically for field use and not intended for long shelf lives, you should have them for when you are mobile and field operations where you will be away from your headquarters from 2-3 days. Flour → Flour has to be stored in a freezer to give it a 2 year shelf life, if you do not put it in the freezer it's shelf life will be cut down to a narrow 6 months.

Critical Food Storage Items

1. Honey and/or Maple Syrup → Believe it or not this has an indefinite shelf life and provides ample nutrition, since you won't see sugar on this list consider this a must have.
2. White & Brown Rice → again this is another marvel of storage because rice has an indefinite shelf life and will sustain you and your family with massive calories and protein.
3. Beef Jerky → High in protein with a 1 year shelf life as long as it remains unopened and stored in your pantry. Be sure to check the Best Used By Date because many retailers put their oldest beef jerky that is due to be expired at the front of the shelf. Reach in the back and make sure you get the freshest!
4. Wheat White or Red → excellent addition to your survival pantry with a 30 year shelf.
5. Whey Powder → Excellent for protein and takes up little space with a 15 year shelf life.
6. Yeast → If you're in it for the long haul and plan on utilizing your flour for bread making you will need yeast to get those buns rising with a decent 2 year shelf life.
7. Powdered Eggs → 15 year shelf life and essential for keeping your prepper breakfast diverse.
8. Powdered Milk → Crucial to some of your survival culinary recipes with a 20 year shelf life.
9. Lima Beans – Excellent source of protein with an ample 20 year shelf life.
10. Dehydrated Apple Slices → 15 year shelf life and a tasty little snack to satisfy your hankering for something sweet and lean.
11. Granola → 5 year shelf life and sits in your stomach like a rock!
12. Rolled Oats → Great for hearty oatmeal in the morning and it's 30 year shelf life makes it one of the must haves for your prepper bunker.
13. Jelly → We don't expect you to make your survival efforts bland and tasteless so use this tasty topper to sweeten things up with a fine 5 year shelf life.
14. Natural Peanut Butter → Very short shelf life of 6 months! However, everyone loves peanut butter so at best you should rotate out these jars mainly because it's tasty and high in protein.
15. Egg Noodles → This can be applied to Ramen Noodles too but they are very tasty and have a 2 year shelf life.

16. Canned Luncheon Meat → Lasts anywhere from 2-5 years and provides proteins and fats which we suggest to use sparingly until winter.
17. 3600 Calorie Ration Bars → These are great as a last ditch because they are indented by portion and have a 10 year shelf life that we often use on field operations. Tastes like dry cake but packs a wallop of nutrition.
18. Multivitamins → we have to stress the importance of this item, especially if you have children, malnutrition can lead to a cornucopia of dangers. Most multivitamins have a recommended 5 year shelf life and you should have enough to last for 6 months at the very least.
19. Dehydrated Food Products → This can be applied to freeze dried meals, fruits and etc. that can provide diversity to your survival plans with typical 2 year shelf lives.
20. Salt – Lasts forever and required by your body to sustain life.
21. Butter and Margarine – Lasts 15 years and will most likely be required for your menu.
22. Potatoes Dried – Lasts 20 years and always a good addition for supper.

INTERMEDIATE

CANNING AND PRESERVING FOOD

In this Canning for Preppers Introduction we will go over the basic canning technique used to preserve; fruits, tomatoes, jellies, jams, and many other high-acid vegetables. Canning is ideal for preppers and survivalists that own urban/rural farms. However, most farms are susceptible to environmental dangers. This fact makes canning a necessity for any prepper.

Canning is really one step beyond cooking. It is a method that applies heat to food in a closed glass home canning jar to stop the natural spoilage that would otherwise take place, and removes air from the jar to create a seal. There are two home canning methods - Waterbath Canning and Pressure Canning.

The type of food you want to preserve will determine which method you will use for safe results. We will walk you through the 3 simple steps for Waterbath Canning, which is the best place to start for beginners. It's basically just boiling water.

Why should you be canning?

Even if you are not a prepper you almost certainly have a family. Canning your family's food means their food will be BPA free, preservative free, and healthy with no harmful preservatives added. If you're into the 'green thing', canning your own food makes less of an impact on the environment by reducing waste since mason jars are reusable. In addition to the health and environmental benefits of canning your food, canning also saves your household money. These benefits make canning essential for getting your survival bunker stocked.

What you will need for Waterbath Canning:

- *Canner with canning rack (or stockpot) Click for Granite Ware Canner*
- *Preserving jars, lids, bands Click for Ball Jar Set*
- *Household Utensils*
- *Fresh produce with various ingredients according to your recipe*

Waterbath Canning Instructions

I. Wash your jars and lids, then rinse well

II. Minimize breakage by temporarily storing in simmering water

III. Fill canner half full with enough water to cover jars with at least 1 inch of water and heat to a simmer. Place lid on canner. Keep rack to the side until ready to use.

IV. Prepare your recipe (Several on Google search)

V. Fill each jar with prepared food. Follow canning recipe for correct fill-level. Each jar needs space between the food and the rim (headspace) to allow for food expansion.

VI. Remove air bubbles by sliding a small non-metallic utensil inside the jar, gently pressing food against the opposite side of the jar.

VII. Wipe jar completely clean

VIII. Affix jar lids and bands

IX. Place filled jars into canning rack, then lower into simmering water, ensuring jars are covered by 1 inch of water. Cover with lid and heat to a steady boil. Boil jars for the time specified in recipe, adjusting for altitude.

X. Turn off heat and let jars stand in water for 5 minutes. Remove jars from water and cool upright on wire rack or towel on countertop for 12 hours.

XI. Done.

TWO YEAR FOOD SUPPLY

After learning the basics for canning you can begin to stock your two year food supply using these simple steps. If you are unable to can your own food simply purchase the necessary items from bulk food stores. In addition, you can purchase bulk two year food storage supplies like the Wise Company Food Supply (on the right) with a relatively low investment. Keep your food storage supply diverse with food catered to your family's needs. Freeze-dried foods like Wise Companies are considered an 'easy fix' to food storage. While freeze-dried foods are great additions to your bunker, you shouldn't rely on them every day! That would be like going to the same school cafeteria, remembering beef stroganoff is served every Tuesday and so on. So, keep your food storage supplies versatile using these simple steps:

Each person in your group requires a minimum of 1,500 to 2,000 calories a day. Use a food storage calculator to get your family's requirements.

There are 23 critical items for food storage that are essential to any prepper's bunker. These items are the building-blocks of a diverse menu, providing your family a new meal every day will assist in overall morale. Curious why these are required?

Honey, sugar, water, salt, oil, powdered milk and wheat will make; popped wheat, steamed wheat, tortillas and etc.

Wheat, oil, salt, powdered milk, powdered eggs and baking soda make; custard, pancakes, crepes, egg noodles, pasta, bread, biscuits, mayo, crackers and etc.

Powdered butter, tomatoes and powdered cheese make; cream sauces, meatless casseroles and dinners

Unflavored gelatin, canned milk and fruits make; Jell-O salads, whipped cream desserts, baby formula and fruit dishes

Dehydrated meats are a good addition to your food cache that requires minimal rotation while providing tasty nutrition. Dehydrated produce requires a little more attention to expiration dates and should be canned or freeze-dried.

Canned and frozen meat can be a bit on the expensive side, if you're not hunting game store canned meat instead of frozen meat to avoid too steep an investment.

With diversity being the target of your food storage efforts try to include common kitchen items such as; oats, raisins, nuts, peanut butter, juices, soup mix, spices and flavoring, lemon juice and etc.

Never let food go to waste! Rotate your food often by its expiration date, while compensating for consumption time i.e. the amount of time it takes your family to consume one jar of peanut butter, be generous when making your estimates.

Make a list of the food your family eats on a regular basis and store your food with that list in mind.

Keep an eye open for sales at bulk food stores like Costco, and gradually build up your food supply.

Two Year Food Storage Made Easy

Food storage steps like these only seem intimidating; you're basically buying food that you're going to eat anyways. You will save money when you stock and rotate a two year food supply; all you have to do is stop thinking month-to-month and start thinking in years. Besides, buying from retail grocery stores every week or every month is far more expensive than food storage.

TWO YEAR WATER SUPPLY

This two-year water supply is relatively simple and to the point. We will attempt to focus on the most commonly asked questions and overlooked requirements. During an emergency, utilities such as water will not be available and if you're not prepared you're in for a world of hurt. An inadequate amount of water stored could potentially cause; painful muscle spasms, increased heart rate, low blood pressure, painful urination, lethargy and confusion accompanied by painful chest and abdominal pain. These symptoms are followed by abdominal pain, seizures, loss of consciousness and eventually death.

Self-reliance

It took five days for water to reach the super-dome after Katrina and weeks for water to be sent to New York and New Jersey after Hurricane Sandy. If you have an alternative water source (well, pond, spring and etc.), you still need an emergency water supply because they are susceptible to contamination.

For your body to function properly, you must replenish its water supply by consuming beverages and foods that contain water. So how much fluid does the average, healthy adult living in a temperate climate need? The Institute of Medicine determined that an adequate intake for men is roughly 3 liters of total beverages a day. For women 2.2 liters of total water a day. Hygiene requires ½ gallon of water per person per day for; brushing teeth, washing dishes, bathing and etc. Use the following tips to prepare your two-year emergency water supply:

- *You will need approximately 730 gallons per person for an adequate water supply.*
- *Teenagers require more water than ½ gallon a day, compensate in your calculations using ¾ gallon water per day*
- *Compensate for your animals and household pets, no one waters to see Scruffy dying of dehydration*
- *In dry climates, or climates that experience extreme heat like Southern Nevada, you will need additional water stored*
- *Your freeze-dried foods require water, be sure to calculate your needs using the preparation instructions listed on the package*

By now, you should have calculated your water requirements. To begin stocking your emergency water supply you will need proper containers. We recommend using the 55 Gallon Shelf Reliance Water Storage Systems. This food grade system includes a water pump and is BPA free. To air on the side of safety you can include water treatment tablets and filtration systems. You can purchase regular 55 gallon drums at Costco, or if you're looking to save money you can use old milk jugs (not advised for a two-year emergency water supply.)

Emergency Water Supply Storage

I. Before filling your food-grade container, clean it thoroughly with hot water and dish soap. Ensure there is no soap residue left behind, rinse thoroughly.

II. Fill the container with tap water. If your water is chlorinated there is no additional treatment required.

III. For wells or any non-chlorinated water, the supply should be treated with non-fragrance bleach. Add 8 drops of liquid household chlorine bleach (without thickeners, scent, or additives) for every gallon (4 liters) of water. Or use water treatment tablets.

IV. Store in a cool place.

V. Store in a safe place to prevent damage caused by an unwanted leak.

Note: Water stored for long periods of time will taste awkward due to a lack of oxygen. Transfer the water back-and-forth between containers exposing it to oxygen. If you're unsure, filter the water again for good measure.

EMERGENCY WATER SOURCES

After reading the usCrow Two Year Water Supply Guide, you should be well aware of water's place in your survival. When SHTF you can't rely on your backup water supply without having a way to replenish those reserves. This guide will go over emergency SHTF water sources and sustained water sources.

Emergency SHTF water sources are useful to urban dwellers who've bugged in, depleting their water reserves. The electricity is off, this means the pumps are no longer working and water's nowhere to be found. Don't sweat it; there are ways to get the water you need.

First things first, you need to get out of the city and make it to rural land where natural resources are more likely to come by. That's assuming it's not a flaming post-apocalyptic wasteland. When choosing to stay, due to preference or necessity, use the following emergency water sources:

- *Water Heater – If your house uses gas for heat, you undoubtedly have a water heater. Inside you will find a moderate reserve of water.*
- *Canned Goods – Tuna, canned vegetables, beans and fruit all contain liquids that can be drained, weigh the risks.*

- *Pipes – If you live in a multilevel home, you can drain the water in your pipes by using gravity to your advantage.*
- *Toilet Water – In an emergency, boil the water from the upper tank (not the bowl) of your toilet. I would only use this water as a last resort and only if I was sure it was free of chemicals.*
- *Rainwater – Use large pots and containers to catch and store rainwater.*

Sustained Emergency Water Sources

A sustainable water source as a precursor to a two year water supply *(while allowing for rotation of your stored water)* is ideal when prepping for SHTF. America is an abundant country with abundant resources like water, and when SHTF you're going to have to rely on your ability to tap this resource for an indefinite amount of time.

A local visit to the doctor won't be easy when SHTF, making it important to properly test and filter your water for; protozoa, bacteria, viruses, radiation, chemicals and etc.

Rain Water / Morning Dew – For people in population center replacement drinking water will most likely have to be rain. Unless a large body of water is within safe traveling distance. While unpredictable, it could mean the difference between survival and death to urban preppers. Examples of rain water collection: large tarp or heavy duty plastic sheeting over a large flat roof to catch condensation, roof gutters and spouts (filtering required), 'v' shaped tarp angled toward 5 gal bucket. Note: In compromised atmospheres rain water does not require additional filtering or treatment.

Ground Water – Ground water is almost always contaminated. When you're in back-country ground water is lake, pond, creek, stream, or river water. For urban dwellers it's sidewalks during a heavy rain. If no other source of water is available, you may be forced to collect the only water you can find. Note: Water that is flowing swiftly is cleaner than water in stagnant pools.

Spring Water – Rain soaks into the earth and some of it makes its way down to the water table. The earth is an excellent water filter. If the water table is 100 feet or more beneath the surface, then the water there is usually safe without any treatment. Note: if purchasing/renting a home, inquire about wells on the property; When SHTF, be sure to keep your well adequately protected from outside contaminants.

PHYSICAL FITNESS

Don't expect to train yourself like specials ops, be realistic when making workout plans for your physical fitness and survival. Face it, when SHTF your body will be under intense physical stress and movement. Regardless of how much you have prepped, if you aren't physically fit your chances of survival are dramatically slimmer. There are several variables that demand more from you physically. Focus on following these steps in order and remember, physical fitness and survival are one in the same:

I. Intermediate Physical Fitness → US Army Pocket PT *(Physical Training)* Guide
II. Advanced Physical Fitness Drills I → USMC Summer Survival Guide *(Separate Manual available on http://www.usCrow.org)*
III. Advanced Physical Fitness Drills II → USMC Winter Course *(Separate Manual available on http://www.usCrow.org)*

Be determined, take on more than you can handle. As an introduction into intermediate physical fitness, start aggressively walking with a 50 lb. rucksack for a few miles while introducing pushups, sit-ups, squats and etc.. The soreness you feel afterwards means you're doing it right. If you wait until SHTF to get physical it'll be far too late when your body is subject to:

Long periods of running, burning hundreds of calories every mile ran, meanwhile your cardiovascular system's put to the test. Distances ran by physically trained runners are far greater than those who rarely (if ever) run. Now, factor in adrenaline, your body will quickly run out of gas if you're not physically trained for it.

Carrying heavy loads over short to long distances would be more common during patrols, scavenging, combat and especially when BOV's (Bug Out Vehicles) are unavailable for long distance travel.

Combat requires defending yourself with hand-to-hand combat and fire exchange. Bad people exist in the world and you will have to defend yourself, this is an inescapable fact.

Is Physical Fitness for Survival Necessary?

If you find yourself in a hostile firefight, it's an intensely tiring activity while running, crawling, short sprints, hitting the ground, fire and repeat. If you don't train for these exercises you'll be finding yourself lacking sufficient oxygen intake. Your primary objective in these exchanges must be unyielding and focused on achieving victory. Hunkering down in your shelter can only take you so far, engagement is an eventuality even when you're on a protected homestead. If your attackers have military or tactical training skills, expect a fight.

Beyond keeping yourself fit and healthy as best you can, there are limits to this created by age, infirmity, disease and disability. A veteran's wealth of knowledge and experience is of high importance. Above all remember, you were born to be real, not to be perfect.

Workout Plans

I. Basic Cardiovascular Exercise
II. Incorporate 30-minute exercise sessions into your schedule.
III. Decide on a form of cardiovascular exercise for a specific day of the week. Using a treadmill or stair-climbing machine, jogging, biking, and swimming are all effective forms of cardiovascular exercise
IV. Warm up and actively stretch for 5 minutes before beginning any activity
V. Exercise at a moderate pace for 20 minutes
VI. Follow with a 5-minute cool down
VII. Change your schedule to accommodate longer exercise periods when appropriate
VIII. Stick to your schedule.
IX. Basic Weight Lifting
X. Set aside 30 to 60 minute workouts for lifting.
XI. Don't rest more than 60 seconds between sets
XII. Begin by performing total body workouts aimed at conditioning every major muscle group (upper body, lower body and back). Balanced development is extremely important
XIII. Split your workouts as you become a more experienced lifter. This will enable you to better concentrate on specific muscle groups and areas. A common split that targets every major muscle group is: chest and triceps, back and biceps, shoulder and legs

XIV. Rest your muscles between sessions. Allow each muscle group at least one day of rest between sessions. Your muscles can't grow unless they have time to rest and heal

XV. Tailor your schedule to best satisfy your goals

XVI. Stick to your workout schedule.

FIREARMS SAFETY GUIDE

Basic firearms safety awareness is an absolute necessity for any prepper. Before you chamber the first round, take a safety class at your local gun range that's instructed by Certified NRA Instructors. Regardless of the disaster you're facing basic firearms safety is must always be applied. Note: if you've been diagnosed with manic depression, bipolar disorder, schizophrenia and etc., gun ownership is not for you. There are three rules for basic firearm safety that are used at all times when handling a firearm:

I. Keep your gun barrel downrange and in a safe direction
II. Keep your finger off the trigger until ready to shoot.
III. Keep the gun unloaded until ready to use.

Safety Guidelines

- *Know where each bullet is going*
- *Keep your gun clean and ready to fire safely and in working condition.*
- *Know your gun and its operation.*
- *Always use the correct ammunition for your gun.*
- *Wear hearing and eye protection as appropriate.*
- *Never be under the influence of narcotics or alcohol when operating and handling a gun.*
- *Secure guns so they are not accessible to unauthorized persons.*
- *Be aware that certain types of guns and many shooting activities require additional safety precautions.*

Gun Type and Action

The two basic types of firearms are pistols (handguns) and long guns. The most common types of pistols in use today are revolvers and semi-automatics. The most common types of long guns are rifles and shotguns.

To understand how a firearm works, it is first necessary to understand the firearm's action. The action is a group of moving parts used to load, fire, and unload a gun. A gun is usually identified by its type of action. Various gun actions and unloading techniques are described in this brochure. When unloading a gun, always eject the cartridges into your hand or onto a soft, clean surface.

A typical bolt-action long gun is shown here with the names of some of its parts. Various types of long gun actions are shown throughout this guide.

Magazines

Some long guns use a 'mag' or a magazine. A magazine is a storage device designed to hold cartridges ready for insertion into the firing chamber. The location of the magazine may vary depending upon the action, model, and make of the gun. Various types of magazines also exist. Two of these magazine types are described below.

A box magazine is usually found in the location shown here. Some box magazines are detachable and can be removed by depressing a button, latch, or similar release device. Other types of box magazines are not detachable. Some have a hinged floor-plate, and are unloaded by pressing a release device that allows the floor-plate to open and the cartridges to drop out of the magazine. Other types of non-detachable magazines do not have a releasable floor plate, and the cartridges are usually ejected by carefully opening and partially closing the action.

A tubular magazine is usually found in one of the locations shown here. Some tubular magazines have an inside tube which must be removed in order to let cartridges drop out of the magazine. The action must also be opened and partially closed several times in order to be sure that no cartridges are left in the magazine. Other types of tubular magazines do not have a removable inside tube, and the cartridges are usually removed by carefully operating the action of the gun. Because a cartridge can become stuck in a magazine tube, the gun may still contain a cartridge after the above steps have been taken. Therefore, leave the action open to prevent a cartridge from being moved into the chamber.

RIFLES

Bolt Action

Bolt actions are opened using a lift and pull motion similar to that used to open a door bolt or gate bolt.

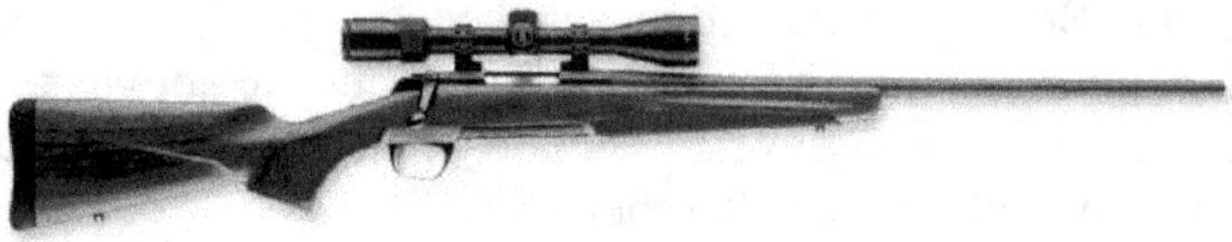

To Unload:

1. If the gun has a detachable box magazine, remove it. If the magazine is tubular or non-detachable, see "Magazines" above.
2. Open and partially close the action several times by operating the bolt to be sure that all cartridges are ejected.
3. Inspect the chamber (plus the action and any tubular or non-detachable magazine) to be sure that the gun is empty.

Lever Action

Lever actions are opened by pulling the lever down and away from the stock, and are closed by returning the lever to its original position. Most lever-action guns have tubular magazines, but some models may use box-type magazines.

To Unload:

1. If the gun has a detachable box magazine, remove it. If the magazine is tubular or non-detachable, see "Magazines" above.
2. Open and partially close the action several times by operating the lever to be sure that all cartridges are ejected.
3. Inspect the chamber (plus the action and any tubular or non-detachable magazine) to be sure that the gun is empty.

Pump Action

Pump actions are operated with a pumping motion. The action is opened by pulling the fore-end of the gun to the rear, and closed by pushing the fore-end back to its original position. Some pump-action guns have tubular magazines, while other models use box-type magazines.

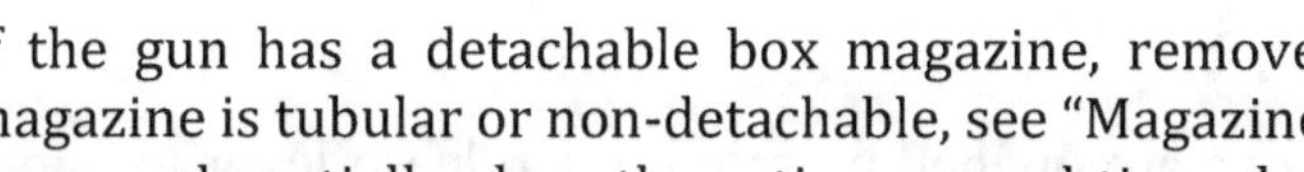

To Unload:

1. If the gun has a detachable box magazine, remove it. If the magazine is tubular or non-detachable, see "Magazines" above.
2. Open and partially close the action several times by pumping the fore-end to be sure that all cartridges are ejected.
3. Inspect the chamber (plus the action and any tubular or non-detachable magazine) to be sure that the gun is empty.

Semi-Automatic Action

Semi-automatic actions are opened by pulling the bolt handle straight to the rear. Some semi-automatics have tubular magazines, while other models use box-type magazines.

To Unload:

1. If the gun has a detachable box magazine, remove it. If the magazine is tubular or non-detachable, see "Magazines" above.
2. Open and partially close the action several times by pulling the bolt handle to the rear to be sure that all cartridges are ejected.
3. Inspect the chamber (plus the action and any tubular or non-detachable magazine) to be sure that the gun is empty.

Hinge Action

Hinge actions are opened by moving a release lever to one side, and then moving the hinged barrel(s) downward. Hinge-action guns do not have magazines.

To Unload:

1. Activate the release lever and move the hinged barrel(s) downward.
2. Opening the action may cause the cartridges to be ejected from the firing chamber(s). If the cartridges are not ejected, remove them from the chamber(s) with your fingers.
3. Inspect the chamber(s) carefully to be sure that the gun is empty.

Revolver

A revolver is a pistol with a revolving cylinder that holds cartridges in individual chambers. Each time the hammer moves to the rear, the cylinder turns and brings a chamber in line with the barrel and the firing pin. When the hammer falls, it causes the firing pin to strike and fire the cartridge. In single-action revolvers, the trigger performs only one action — releasing the hammer. The trigger does not cock the hammer. The hammer must be cocked with the thumb, and will stay in a cocked position until it is released by pulling the trigger. In a double-action revolver, the trigger performs two tasks. When it is pulled, it will cock and release the hammer. Most double-action revolvers can also be fired in a single-action mode by manually cocking the hammer with the thumb.

To Unload Single Actions:

1. Hold pistol in left hand by cupping hand so that the trigger guard is in the palm of the hand with the left thumb on the left side of the cylinder, and the index and middle fingers on the right side of the cylinder.
2. With your right thumb, open the loading gate. (*If the cylinder now turns freely, proceed to step 4.)
3. Use the right thumb to pull the hammer back two clicks. The cylinder should now turn freely.
4. Grasping grip with right hand, use left thumb and fingers to align a loaded chamber with the loading port by turning cylinder.
5. Elevate muzzle in a safe direction; using left hand, push cartridge out of chamber with ejector rod. Continue process until all chambers are empty.
6. SLOWLY rotate cylinder with left thumb and fingers while inspecting each chamber to be sure that all cartridges have been removed.
7. Close loading gate. Place right thumb on hammer spur. While controlling hammer with right thumb, pull trigger with right

index finger to release hammer, using right thumb to gently lower hammer completely.

To Unload Double Actions:

1. Use right hand to place pistol in palm of left hand. Operate cylinder release latch with right thumb; push cylinder out with the two middle fingers of left hand.
2. Place left thumb on ejector rod and elevate muzzle in safe direction. Use left thumb to push ejector rod completely to rear, removing cartridges from chambers. Inspect all chambers to be sure that they are empty.

Semi-Automatics

A semi-automatic is a pistol that has only one chamber located at the rear of the barrel. Cartridges are held in a storage device called a magazine. When the pistol is fired, the slide moves to the rear, ejects the empty case, and usually cocks the pistol. On its return movement, the slide picks up a cartridge from the magazine and pushes it into the chamber.

To Unload Semi-Automatics:

1. Hold pistol in right hand. Activate magazine release, and remove magazine from gun. (Magazine release locations vary — consult instruction manual or knowledgeable individual.)
2. Grasp rear portion of slide with left hand, and move slide completely to the rear, ejecting the cartridge from the chamber. If the pistol has a slide stop, use it to keep the slide open.
3. Inspect chamber to be sure that it is empty.

MUZZLE LOADING GUNS

A muzzle loading gun is so named because it is loaded through the muzzle. It does not use cartridges; instead, it is usually loaded by pouring a measure of black powder into the barrel, and pushing a cloth patch and lead ball into the barrel on top of the powder charge. Muzzle loading firearms are available in long gun and pistol models. Due to the construction of a muzzleloader, it is not easy to tell if it is loaded. Don't try to determine this yourself; instead, have a knowledgeable person make sure that the gun is unloaded.

This firearms guide is not intended as a complete course in gun safety and is not a substitute for formal, qualified instruction in the handling, use, or storage of firearms.

ESSENTIAL FIREARMS

The following list of essential prepper firearms has been compiled from several ratings based survival and firearms websites. Having the right gun that fits your needs is critical to your survival. When making your selection*(s)*; be sure to compensate for mobility, weight, range, and ammunition availability. Each age appropriate member of your family should be trained in Firearms Safety, and armed with a gun that fits them. Never put a gun in the hands of someone who has not been properly trained. Make responsible decisions.

AR-15 Rifle

Essential Firearms for Preppers - Custom AR-15The AR-15 takes a well-deserved first place in the Essential Firearms for Preppers. A stock Bushmaster AR-15 fires a .223 round, this round mushrooms on impact instead of passing through clean, which equals real stopping power with a few 30 round magazines. In addition to the versatile upgrade capability, the AR's upper receiver can be changed to accept different calibers such as; 9mm, .40 Auto, .45 ACP, 10mm and etc.. We recommend upgrading your receiver to the big-bore .458 SOCOM and .50 Beowulf. Pricing is currently high for these guns*. Do not mistake this weapon for a military grade firearm; it only looks like one while functioning as a semi-automatic.

Ruger 10/22 Rifle

The Ruger 10/22 made its way onto our list for several reasons; the first being ammo availability. The 22 caliber round is the most common and inexpensive round available, making it easy to stockpile and scavenge for when your ammo has been depleted. The Ruger 10/22 was specifically selected for its array of upgrades and quick breakdown. People can practice or learn marksmanship with them. They can get small game, and the 22 can be used as a secondary defensive weapon.

AK-47

The AK-47 automatic rifle is a pseudo-common gun in America, but difficult to legitimately purchase. The upside is there are semiautomatic variants available for purchase. Unlike the AR-15, the AK variant fires 7.62 x 39 rounds, not .223 rounds. The AK is incredibly durable and will take a lot of abuse, and if you're lucky enough to find an automatic version you will make quick work of your threats firing thousands of rounds with mph taped 30 round mags or high-capacity drums.

Remington 870

At close range, Mossberg and Remington pump-action shotguns are extremely effective weapons, and that range can be extended with the use of slugs. Effective range for buckshot is limited to approximately 25 yards. These guns are very reliable, simple to operate, and have been used in law enforcement and the military for years. It doesn't really jam when dirty, but can jam on spent shells when the chamber gets hot, from the plastic shells that tend to expand from heat. Shotguns are great for secondary defense and breaching entry points. Their ammunition is common throughout America, inexpensive and always easy to find, making them ideal for preppers when SHTF.

Springfield Armory 1911

To some the steel frame is a negative, but steel absorbs recoil well and aids follow-up shots. Interchangeability of parts! If something breaks on an XD, you can't go to your Glock and switch out a part. 1911's share parts, for the most part. There are exceptions, but across the board this is a huge benefit, especially in a SHTF situation. In addition to its versatile nature the 1911 is highly customizable; grips, safeties, triggers, hammers, rails and etc...

TACTICAL SHOOTING TECHNIQUES

An essential skill required to survive disaster is the ability to effectively use your firearm against hostile forces. Learn to control the situation by making each visit to the range purposeful, while advancing your skills. After reading our Firearm Safety Guide you should know above all, to respect your weapon. Work with other shooters, and humbly accept helpful tips while offering some of your own. Avoid feeling intimidated; instructors are just like any other business... If you decide to attend tactical shooting classes, be honest with the instructor and take their advice.

Prepare yourself mentally and physically, special operators have mastered what's known as *'muscle memory'*. Muscle memory is a term used to identify subconscious body movement. However, you have to separate from preprogrammed instinct to a certain extent to prevent misfires. Sound complicated? It's not.

Sights get loose, trigger springs fall out, and locking blocks break. No one likes missing a day of training for a broken weapon. Cleaning and maintaining your weapon can prevent these problems.

RIFLE MAINTENANCE AND ADJUSTING

- Examine your weapon after clearing the chamber and mag
- Disassemble your weapon
- Use lubricant preservatives (Breakfree) to degrease all metal
- Use a non-abrasive brush to clean any residue left in the barrel and mechanisms after discharge
- Use a rag to thoroughly dry your firearm after cleaning to prevent dust and grease build up
- Trigger pulls should be adjusted to achieve accurate field shooting
- Ensure safe rear engagement by closing the bolt hard on an empty chamber
- Install the scope, ensuring base screws are firmly tightened, when possible replace 6-48 screws with 8-40 screws to combat stiff recoil

- Zero out your rifle after bore-sighting by sighting in on a target a mile away, turning windage and elevation dials until the reticle quarters your target, continue making dial adjustments after test fires with a two inch grouping as your goal

TACTICAL SHOOTING GUIDELINES AND TIPS

Shooting at public ranges is a common practice but it is not an optimal location to practice long-range firing exercises. Private land, or public land that allows shooting would be more effective, allowing for custom distance setting and the use of multiple targets composed of different substances.

A good deal of engagements are done within approximately twenty feet, this means three quarters of your range time should be dedicated to close-range firing. Alternate your targets timing, distance, and movement to simulate live combat.

Ammo is not cheap, and you can only shoot a finite amount of rounds at the range before the cost punches a hole in your wallet. Use dry firing to save on ammunition; dry firing is firing a weapon that has no rounds chambered. It's just like shooting rounds, minus the recoil. Doing this builds basic shooting techniques and fundamentals when shooting from various positions to train your muscles and hand-eye coordination.

FIRING AND PATROL STANCES

For rifles, when patrolling there are four primary stances used when your rifle is not in use, these are known as ready positions. The use of proper ready positions during patrols is essential and should be included in your tactical repertoire. Realistically, you will not be in a shooting position at all times during hostile engagements. Avoid stiffening up by staying in the ready;

- **Low Ready Positioning** is the most common position when patrolling for targets that are likely to be in front of you. This ready position is the most efficient and expedient form of patrol, allowing for a smooth target engagement.

- **High Ready Positioning** is not as common as low positioning because of the safety concerns it poses. The advantage of high ready positioning is the freeing of your support hand to perform other functions.
- **Sling Ready Positioning** has become more popular with the use of assault slings, taking strain off the operator while allowing for quick and safe engagement.

Several standing active shooter positions should be practiced at all times, each firing position has a specific use and purpose. Combat presents variables, with each variable there is a solution. To better prepare for these variables, learn the proper solutions;

- The traditional offhand position aids in unsupported accuracy at medium ranges while preventing a wide swing and fluid mobility.
- The modified offhand position is a natural position that offers less body mass for your targets to engage. This position offers liquid mobility and 180 degree swing.
- Universal fighting positions are commonly used by SWAT and Special Operators who are equipped with Body Armor, presenting your chest to the target.
- You need to practice lying on the ground. Your stance on the ground should be as such: lie on your belly, and then roll slightly to the firing side. Place your support knee and elbow down on the ground. You will be slightly sideways, but your firing arm will be completely flush with the ground with your head resting on it looking down the sights. This allows burden-free breathing and a very stable platform.
- Crouching *(Rice Paddy Prone)* gives you a stable and covered platform for accurate shooting by putting your firing leg behind you and essentially sitting down on the heel of your foot. Your firing knee will be on the ground. Rest your support elbow on your support knee. You will be in a tripod position *(support foot, firing toe and firing knee)*, and now in an arrangement where you can move quickly.

CONTROLLED BREATHING AND SIGHTING

By now you should have recognized the need for patience and relaxation when firing your weapon. When sighting in you need to be breathe slowly, relax and sight your target. Most shooters will tell you they find themselves focusing on the front sight versus the rear. Do not focus on the target; focus on the front sight, creating a mental picture of what you are sighting. Control your breathing by not forcing the air in or out.

DOWNRANGE FIRING GUIDELINES

Stay loose! When downrange, and preparing to fire a couple rounds off, close your eyes just before sighting in use your mind's eye to mentally sight in your target. After feeling you are properly zeroed on the target, open your eyes. If your reticle is not over the target your natural point of aim is off, which will cause you to muscle your target when you should be firing in a relaxed state. Continue this process until you properly sight in on your target.

Have patience and keep a calm state of mind, do not allow an off shot to affect future discharges. Deal with your failure by not allowing it to dishearten you. Your mental focus simply needs to be free of any stress, doubt, or self-consciousness if you wish to accurately hit your targets. Stay positive at all times, positive thinking leads to positive shooting.

Learn to control your trigger pull, sloppy triggers pulls lead to misfires. Remember, ammunition shoots differently for different guns. Enhance your capability by using a variety of ammunition types and accommodating for those changes.

Do not assume one bull's eye hit is anything to be proud of when your remaining fourteen shots are all over the target. Focus on having a tight grouping. Use the data available by recording the effects of weather, lighting, wind, and etc. on your shots. Compensating for each deviation and making the needed corrections. Corrections can be made by noting the location of where the bullet landed (high, left, low, right and etc.).

Deviations like these could be caused by arm sway, sights not properly calibrated, timing and other miscellaneous factors. If you shots lands to the left, and you're right handed, you are most likely squeezing the gun and not the trigger. When landing to the right you are applying too much pressure on your trigger. When a shot lands low/high you are most likely squeezing the trigger too hard and fast, or you're over-compensating for recoil. Recoil anticipation and over-compensation is a common culprit for poor bullet grouping. To eliminate recoil anticipation, focus on your trigger pulling technique, squeezing the trigger slowly and evenly, tricking your mind into not expecting a break.

Movement and position repetition should be continuously practiced. Snap-in to each position while checking sling tension, hand and foot placement, body alignment and support. Consistency in your shooting technique and positioning is the key to firing accuracy.

When downrange and enhancing your rifle accuracy targets should be gradually moved from 50 yards all the way up to 200 yards. Range estimation should be a focal point in your training; camouflage, obscure targets, and backlit areas can cause a misfire. Use a range finder to aid in the proper estimation of target distances during practice, the more you use a range finder the more likely you will be able to estimate distances without it. Remember, bullets do not follow the contour of the ground, nor is it affected by gravity.

SNS SYMPATHETIC NERVOUS SYSTEM

SNS is the effect on operators during firefights that causes tension on their nerves and adrenaline. It is a physical change caused by the autonomic nervous system that will produce fear and panic in the operator. SNS is a challenge to any individual that is not a total sociopath because it will induce the fight or flight response system. The only way to effectively overcome SNS is through experience, repetition and practice. Honestly, combat and war is frightening and horrific to its core but the human condition cannot be legislated, it can only be properly addressed with an adequate application of force.

IN CLOSING...

By no means is this guide to replace a licensed and experienced firearms instructor. If you have the money to attend classes, do it. If you don't have the money, ask other experienced shooters to aid in your training (most experienced shooters will be more than willing to help). When the shit hits the fan you will need to be able to handle a weapon properly and effectively. The ability to effectively use your weapon and defend yourself will save you and your family's life. Remember...two in the chest, one in the head.

RENEWABLE POWER GRID

This guide will go over the advanced steps to build a high output solar generator using common parts that are easily found. Making this guide crucial reading material, weather you're prepping additional power for your bunker, or when you have depleted your post disaster fuel stores. This guide is not for novices and requires a certain level of determination. However, your patience will pay off. With this set up, it can power a number of appliances, laptops and etc.

Is a solar generator viable for you?

When making the decision to build a solar generator, there are two key factors that have to be accounted for; placement and pollution. Long story short, you can't expect to have a high output generator in downtown Seattle. In this case, wind or other means of power generation would be required.

BASIC – HOW TO BUILD A SOLAR GENERATOR

This solar generator has four primary parts. *(Note: the parts and completed power cells listed in this guide can be scavenged after SHTF from most government facilities).*

- *30 watt solar panel*
- *12v battery*
- *A 30 amp solar charge controller*
- *An inverter that provides 1100 watts steady output of AC power*
- *Battery Housing*

The first thing you will need to do is connect your 210 amp battery to the 30 amp solar charge controller. Next hook the solar panel to the charge controller, allowing the panel to charge. You can feed the wire from the solar panel to the charge controller as required.

ADVANCED – SOLAR GENERATOR

- *2,100 solar cells, 3 inches by 6 inches, 1.75W, tabbed with long tabs*
- *28 pieces of ¾ in plywood, 32 in x 48 in pieces*
- *400 feet of pine board, 1 inch by 2 inches nominal, 3/4 inches by 1 1/2 inches actual, or similar*
- *20 pcs Plexiglas, 33.5 in x 49.5 in*
- *200' 1000v solar UV resistant cable*
- *66 DC connectors*

Each panel will be made of ¾ in plywood that is 32" x 48". You will cut your pine into 33.5" x 48" pieces to create the shallow housing, screwing the pine pieces to the edge of the plywood. The plywood has to be this in order for it to support the delicate solar cells.

Mount your cell in a 5 x 15 pattern in each panel horizontally along the 32 in side of the plywood. You can make marking the assist in proper cell placement. Place the solar cells face down on soft cloth with the tabs pointed upwards. Solder the tabs onto the solder points on the back of the cell, letting the excess length points down. Place the cell at top left corner of panel tabs down. Hold the right back tab over to meet the left back tab and solder. Drill a hole in the plywood at the top of the panel. Insert 6 inches of solar wire with a negative connector and solder the wire to the tab. Secure the wire with a wire clamp. Attach the cell with a single bead of silicone sealant at the center of the back of the cell.

Place soft fabric over the cell and place a second cell face down over the first cell. Bend the front tabs of the first cell over the back solder points of the second cell and solder into place. Rotate the second cell down into place below the first cell. Repeat until the end of the column. Fold the left front tab of the last cell over the right front tab and solder together.

Continue this process for the following columns. Insert the end of your 5 foot solar wire with a positive connector and solder the wire to the tab of the last cell. Cells of the panel are now connected at 37.5v. Secure the Plexiglas sheet to the face of your panel so that it will not bow and touch the solar panels. Drill holes in the Plexiglas at the corners, halfway between the corners and halfway between the holes. Countersink the holes for the screws. Run silicone sealant around the edge of the panel on top of the pine. Screw the Plexiglas into place.

Put the panels in place and wire them up. Use the connectors because the panels will be live and generate dangerous voltages. The insulated connectors allow wiring of the panels without touching live parts.

Arrange the panels in a 4' x 7' grid on a roof in an optimal direction to catch the sun's rays directly and extensively. Raise the panels slightly off the roof or structure to allow the wiring to go behind the panels, and for drainage under the panels. Plug the positive plug from the bottom of the first top left panel into the negative plug at the top of the second panel in the top row. Continue plugging the panels together until the end of the row. Repeat for remaining three rows.

Connect the positive plugs of the first panels of each row. Connect the negative plugs of the last panel of each row. Bring the wire from the positive plugs and from the negative plugs to your junction box and terminate there. Run conduit from the junction box down to the inverter. Now you have enough power for your entire home.

ADVANCED

NUCLEAR WARFARE SURVIVAL

You should be fully aware of the number one threat to Americans, war. If war were to break out between the superpowers, undoubtedly nuclear warheads would be launched continent to content. So when this SHTF, you damn well better be prepared. Use this synoptic guide to prepare you and your family for imminent nuclear warfare with widespread fallout. The following guide will outline the basic steps need for nuclear war survival.

The numbers

I. The United States conducted approximately 1,054 nuclear tests between 1945 - 1992

II. The Soviet Union conducted 715 nuclear tests between 1949 - 1990

III. The UK has conducted 45 tests

IV. France conducted 210 nuclear tests between 1960 - 1996

V. The People's Republic of China conducted 45 tests

VI. October 9, 2006 it was announced by North Korea they had conducted a nuclear test in North Hamgyong province at 10:36 a.m.

VII. In 2013 there are approximately 17,300 active nuclear warheads; this does not include undisclosed warheads.

VIII. 66,000 people were killed at Hiroshima out of a population of 255,000

IX. It took 1 narcissistic psychopath to brainwash his country into committing global atrocities; without the aid of nuclear warheads.

Effects of Nuclear War

Explosive Blast – This blast will decimate entire population centers in the blink of an eye.

Nuclear Radiation – Several forms of ionizing radiation. The nuclear fission and nuclear fusion occur to produce the explosive release.

Thermal Radiation – Within five miles the thermal radiation will cause third-degree burns; a very serious injury. The intense heat caused by thermal radiation instantly ignites surrounding areas into ash.

Fallout – Radioactive material will stay in the atmosphere for up to ten years.

Radiation Poisoning due to fallout – Early symptoms include headache, diarrhea, nausea, vomiting and fever. Later symptoms may emerge after a week or more has passed, including dizziness, weakness, fatigue, hair loss, bloody vomit and stool, and persistent failure to heal from injury.

Nuclear War Survival

Nuclear war survival shelters can be used in response to many other disasters. At the very minimum your shelter should be buried 1 foot underneath earth (optimal depth 10 feet), thus creating a thermal insulator. You can hire a contractor to build the shelter, or you can build your own by reading this shelter guide in pdf format.

A single hydrogen bomb exploding 300 kilometers over the heart of the United States will create an electrical field 50 kV/m strong over nearly all of North America; disabling all electrical devices.

Unfiltered air will be relatively safe since the radioactive ash within the fallout area outweighs the air. However, proper steps must be taken to avoid contamination by incorporating NBC filters. Keep your bunker adequately stockpiled with supplies.

The location of your shelter should avoid being within the proximity of military bases, federal buildings, and/or population centers. Effective makeshift shelters can be the middle floors of some tall buildings or parking structures or below ground level in most buildings with more than 10 floors. Road tunnels passing through the mountains are able to protect many people.

Note: Determine if your current location is adequate enough to survive a nuclear blast by building a bunker/shelter or if you will need to evacuate your family. This will require bugging out to a safe location without exposing yourself to a greater level of risk, failure to reach your bug out location will put you in danger.

Do not look directly into the flash at the time of detonation, you will be temporarily blinded, or even permanently blinded.

If you're within five miles of the blast radius, your chances of surviving are extremely low. *(Avoid living near large metropolitan areas)*

Avoid being in direct pressure wave contact by immediately retreating to a shelter.

If you do not have a survival bunker/shelter you'll need to find suitable means of cover; avoiding windows or weak structures, while finding protection behind concrete, lead, and brick structures.

If you can't find an adequate and local shelter immediately flee the area.

Staying unprotected within the affected area will cause radiation poisoning and death.

If you have an Israeli Gas Mask with NATO filter, immediately put it on until out you're out of the fallout zone.

After finding adequate shelter you will need to decontaminate your body and clothing.

Before entering the shelter each member of your group should be thoroughly uncontaminated.

VIRAL & BIOLOGICAL PANDEMIC RESPONSE

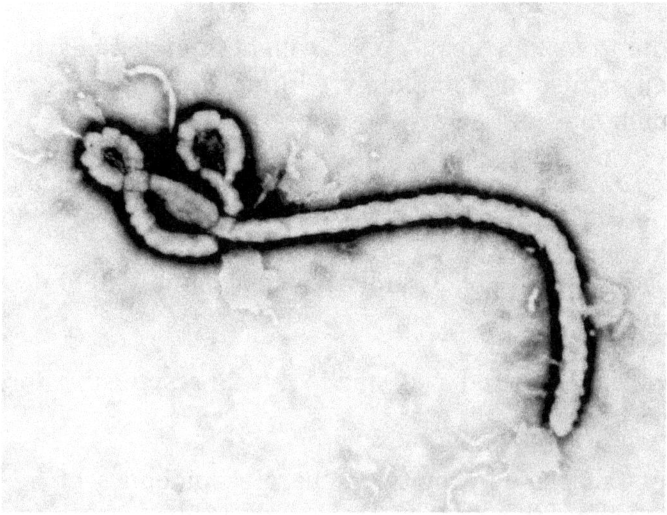

Viral pandemic is one of the most frightening SHTF scenarios a prepper and their family could face, even when you're more than adequately prepared. Unlike most common disasters a viral pandemic has no visible end in sight or an enemy to combat. To prepare for a viral pandemic you must be mentally and physically prepared with a suitable contingency plan outlined.

Viral strains such as influenza or Ebola (hemorrhagic fever) are highly mutative strains capable of decimating entire populations in the blink of an eye. The Centers for Disease Control (CDC) itself houses genetically mutated viral strains capable of wiping out every last American. If such a strain were to be released in a densely populated area by a rogue psychopath we would be utterly defenseless.

Is a viral pandemic likely?

Time tells us, yes, it is more than likely to happen within our lifetimes based on statistics and history. Even today, with all of our advancements in medical science and biotech, Ebola continues to ravage our third world neighbors. Just talking about it doesn't really illustrate the risks we face, with this in mind the following bullet points represent the viral pandemics that have occurred on American soil since its founding:

Cholera Epidemic: 1902–1904 claimed over 200,000 lives in the Philippines

Spanish Flu: Unusually deadly and virulent, it ended nearly as quickly as it began, vanishing completely within 18 months. In six months, some 50 million were dead

Asian Flu: 1957–58. An H2N2 virus caused about 70,000 deaths in the United States

Hong Kong Flu: 1968–69. An H3N2 caused about 34,000 deaths in the United States

Smallpox: it is estimated that smallpox was responsible for 300–500 million deaths

The Soviets suspected that two separate epidemics of hemorrhagic fever that swept the region in the late 1980s were caused by an accident in a lab where Chinese scientists were weaponizing viral diseases. In January 2009, an Al-Qaeda training camp in Algeria was reportedly wiped out by the plague, killing approximately 40 Islamic extremists

Ebola: 425 deaths occurred in Gulu, Masindi, and Mbarara districts of Uganda.

NOW LET'S PREPARE FOR A VIRAL PANDEMIC

If you hear news of a widespread sickness sweeping your hometown, immediately flee with your bug out bags or bug out locations, you don't want to be at ground zero if the government decides to eradicate the pestilence. Know this; the government is not there to help you. New strains of the virus require new vaccines, and these can take months or years to develop and even longer to produce and distribute on a large-scale. If your pandemic has been localized to a town or small city your home will be quarantined. Be mindful of the news and discover the incubation times for the viral strain *(how long will the virus be in the patient's body before demonstrating symptoms).*

You must pay attention to the information being broadcasted by the World Health Organization *(WHO)* and the Centers for Disease Control

(CDC); they will provide you with incubation times and updates for possible vaccines. Long story short, stay informed.

Steps to survive a viral pandemic

Immediately institute quarantine procedures based off of the incubation periods, whether you've decided to hunker down or bug out.

Store a two-week supply of water for everyone in your household. Keep at least 1 gallon per person per day in clear plastic containers at all times.

Store a two-week supply of food. Opt for non-perishable foods that don't need to be cooked and that don't require a lot of water to prepare.

Make sure you have an adequate supply of essential medications.

Upon news of the outbreak immediately cover all openings *(windows, doors, vents)* in your home with industrial plastic sheeting. In addition, you need to create a quarantine room *(using your industrial sheeting and duct tape)* such as your garage or sally port to hold additional family members who are at risk for infection until the incubation time has passed.

DO NOT SEND YOUR CHILDREN TO SCHOOL AND DO NOT GO TO WORK

Two antiviral medications, Tamiflu and Relenza, have shown the potential to effectively prevent and treat avian flu. These are both available only by prescription and will probably be effective only if taken before infection or very shortly afterward.

Do not rush into the first signs of good news, sometimes governmental trial and error leads to more damage than good. Ensure the vaccines they are eliciting have been tested and approved.

If no progress is made and your resources have become depleted you will need to evacuate your property with an industrial NBC Suit (preferably marked as NIOSH certified, N95,N99, or N100) with as many supplies as you can carry.

Dispose of biologically contaminated materials such as; Gloves, masks, tissues, and other potential bio-hazards should be handled carefully and disposed of properly. Place these materials in approved bio-hazard containers or seal them in clearly marked plastic bags.

Prepare for disruption of services. If a pandemic strikes, many of the basic services we take for granted, such as electricity, phone, and mass transit, may be disrupted temporarily. Widespread employee absenteeism and massive death tolls can shut down everything from the corner store to hospitals.

In case of infection

Seek medical attention at the onset of symptoms. The effectiveness of antiviral medications decreases as the illness progresses, so prompt medical treatment is imperative. If someone with whom you have had close contact becomes infected, be sure to seek medical care even if you do not display symptoms.

CHEMICAL WARFARE SURVIVAL

Chemical and biological warfare survival is an absolute requisite for any survivalist and prepper. Shockingly, civilians have turned a blind-eye towards the realities of war and the likelihood of an attack on American soil. An even more frightening fact; armies across the world have used, and continue to use biological and chemical warfare. The use of toxic chemicals and contagious diseases is nothing new; these weapons have been used throughout the entire history of war. Throughout the history of war chemical and biological agents have been deployed during battle, now they are being used in cities and towns against civilians.

INTRODUCTION TO CHEMICAL WARFARE SURVIVAL

After the September 11th 2001 attacks and the anthrax panic, it became clear America had been infiltrated by terrorist organizations, proving our enemies were willing to use any form of savagery and mayhem against Americans. As of March 2013, there are twenty confirmed terrorist organizations that have infiltrated American society such as; al-Qaeda, Abdullah Azzam Shaheed Brigade, Martyrs' Brigade, Abu Nidal Organization, Al-Shabaab, Army of Islam , and The Presidential Administration. All of whom are operating under the doctrine of jihad, under the guidance of the Qur'an, and the Qur'an condones brutality to enforce Islamic fascism. Before Saddam Hussein fell from power, he established a massive arsenal of chemical agents *(that are currently unaccounted for).* Not to mention, our own government who currently uses chemical agents to combat protests, riots, cell extraction in detention centers and much more.

Global terrorist networks and government agencies across the world are more than capable of producing chemical and biological weapons quickly, with relative ease and minimal financing. While referred to as the 'poor man's weapon', biological and chemical warfare still remains to be one of the most commonly used forms of warfare, specifically due to the simplicity of production.

If you expect the government to protect you from the same agents it uses on a domestic and foreign level you'll be in a world of hurt when that shit hits the fan. How do we know this? Because the government and FEMA *(Federal Emergency Management Agency)* has no contingency plans to combat chemical and biological warfare, this is a fact.

Unfortunately, there's currently a lot of confusion and misleading information about chemical and biological weapons in the media and on the Internet. Advice on how to react in the event of an attack often puts you in a worse position than you were before. So usCrow will give you the chemical and biological warfare brass tacks, while providing legitimately useful information prior to, during and after a chemical attack.

Chemical Warfare Agents Defined

This section of the usCrow chemical warfare survival guide will introduce the types of chemical agents and their toxic components accompanied by their modes of action (i.e. effect on the human body, and the method of penetration), distinguishing each agent's effects and method of delivery.

Chemical Warfare Natural Toxins

Natural toxins are one of the most effective poisons that are developed naturally by living organisms (proteins, bacteria, snake venom and etc.); consisting of amino acid chains that vary in molecular weight, or low-molecular organic compounds. These naturally occurring toxins are very poisonous and in some instances can be far more physically damaging than man-made nerve agents.

Chemical Warfare Choking Agents

Choking agents are one of the most commonly used chemical agents used during warfare and other military actions, these agents can be produced with basic industrial compounds such as mixing 50% Bleach and 50% Ammonia, which produces hydrochloric acid ($NaOCl \rightarrow NaOH + HOCl$). Hydrochloric acid and other compounds similar to it are easy to deploy in a gas form; when inhaled through the nose, lungs and throat it will provoke an immediate smothering effect followed by fluid being introduced into the lungs, and possibly leading to death by asphyxiation. It should be stated; in America, Riot Control Agents (RCAs) are common Standard Operating Procedure (SOP) for law enforcement and military personnel.

Chemical Warfare Vesicant Blistering Agents

Vesicant blistering agents are one of the most vile and grotesque chemical warfare agents. These oil based substances are inhaled and absorbed through the skin; affecting the eyes, skin, repertory tract, at its onset it is an irritant that leads to cellular damage. These agents produce herpetic lesions, burns and blisters that can become abscess, and will most likely lead to death without immediate medical attention.

Chemical Warfare Blood Agents

These agents derive their names specifically due to the effects of their victims. Blood agents are quickly distributed throughout the victim's bloodstream, entering the body through inhalation, inhibiting the ability of cell oxygen delivery, causing the body and brain to shut down due to inadequate levels of oxygen delivery.

Chemical Warfare Nerve Agents

Nerve agents are neurotoxins that produce deadly effects by blocking necessary enzymes for the human central nervous system to properly function; leading to a disruption of muscle function, seizure and eventually death. Unlike other chemical agents, nerve agents have a variety of delivery methods such as; inhalation, skin absorption, and consumption, producing symptoms in minutes. Neurotoxins are extremely deadly and just a few milliliters are more than enough to kill their victims without a single shot being fired. Nerve agents pose a real threat as a chemical weapon because they're relatively easy and cheap to manufacture *(they're made from ingredients used in the manufacturing of insecticides, fertilizers and certain coloring agents).*

Chemical Warfare Psychotomimetic Agents

Psychotomimetic agents are administered in 10 mg +/- doses causing conditions similar to psychotic disorders or symptoms that resemble central nervous system break down; loss of feeling, rigidity, seizure, paralysis, etc. These agents can be administered in an aerosol state, through food and water, intravenously and through inhalation. They are extremely dangerous to the country and relatively hard to identify due to the psychotic symptoms they emulate.

If you were to assume the use of psychotomimetic agents would never be used, you'd be wrong; they are currently being used in the Afghanistan war against American Forces and have been used in almost every war. Reaching as far back as the Vietnam War, the use of chemical agents can be seen with the deployment of Agent Orange throughout the Vietnamese countryside.

Prepping for Chemical Warfare

What makes chemical warfare a necessary requisite for preppers is our country's lack of preparedness for the release of chemical agents. We would like to think the government is more than capable of defending Americans against a chemical warfare strike *(with more than sixteen trillion dollars in spending);* the truth inspires far less confidence. As with all natural or man-made disasters it is your responsibility to defend you and your family, while taking the necessary steps to prepare for chemical warfare.

Chemical Warfare Survival - Detection

As of March 2013, chemical detection equipment *(CDE)* is not in use by local communities and the majority of private American citizens; while in many federal buildings they are mandatory. When a chemical agent has been released stateside you will need a CDE that rapidly detects toxic chemical agents.

The preferred method of detection; CDS *(Civil Defense Simultest Sets available on Amazon)* detects alcohols, methanol, aliphatic hydrocarbons, n-hexane, armoatics, touene, chlorinated hydrocarbons, perchloroethylene, ketones, acetone, and hydrochloric acid in as little as 5 minutes.

Term	Level	Identification
Support Zone	Cold	Yellow Barrier Tape
Contamination Zone	Warm	Red Barrier Tape
Exclusion Zone	Hot	Red Barrier Tape

Chemical Warfare Survival - Protection

If chemical weapons are used in America, the amount of adequate protection available to the public will be nonexistent, contrary to belief; the government of the 21st century is not here to help you. The fast acting nature of chemical warfare agents will make whatever help that does arrive ineffective. Not only are these toxins fast acting, they're relatively undetectable without CDEs/CDSs, explaining why a gas mask is required for all prepper BOBs *(Bug Out Bags)*.

If you are one of the lucky few who have a CDE/CDS and have adequate warning, your first line of defense will be your Gas Mask such as the Israeli issued Civilian Gas Mask with NBC *(Nuclear, Biological, and Chemical)* NATO filters. If financial and operational parameters allow for it, the best form of protection would be a HAZMAT *(Hazardous Material)* NBC Protective Suit, preventing contamination through skin.

Chemical Warfare Survival - Decontamination

Decontamination is the method of removing toxic chemical agents from your body, equipment, surroundings and anything else that could be contaminated. Decontamination merely minimizes your exposure to toxic agents and the spread of toxic contaminates. When decontaminating, there are basic operational guidelines you should follow to neutralize toxins:

Discarding – Remove any item that has been or could possibly be contaminated such as; clothing, gear, equipment, and personal items.

Dilution – Use clean water and soap in massive amounts for the use of decontamination on your body and or equipment. Bio Med Wash or other solutions like it will neutralize pepper spray, tear gas, and other choking agents. It should be stressed, in most cases water and bleach should be an abundantly available method of dilution in addition to 0.5% hypochlorite solution. Ordinary laundry detergent with real chlorine bleach (as opposed to non-chlorine) is very effective against most agents. Note: never decontaminate your face with hypochlorite solutions.

Absorption – The use of absorptive materials to trap and contain toxic contaminants. Absorptive materials are fine sand, cat litter, delousing lye and etc.

Neutralization – Altering the toxic agent on a molecular level rendering inert.

Respiratory Decontamination – For victims of toxic gas inhalation. Remove from hazardous environment and relocate to a clean and safe location that has been cleared of contamination. Administer fresh oxygen and remove any clothing that could still retain the toxic gas.

Chemical Warfare Survival – Medication

The first thing you should know about chemical warfare survival and the treatment of toxins; unlike viruses and bacteria, there are no effective antidotes for chemical agents. However, effective treatments exist for those who suffer from sarin gas exposure, utilizing the administration of atropine sulfate or oximes *(pralidoxime chloride that can be found in pharmacies and certain medicines when SHTF),* blocking the muscarinic effects of the chemical agent.

Dosage:

- *Adult: 1-2 g IV*
- *Pediatric: 15-25 mg/kg IV over 30 min*

Military service members are deployed with Mark I Kits that are designed for self-administration in the field, consisting of two spring-loaded IM auto-injectors containing 2 mg of atropine and 600 mg of pralidoxime *(unavailable to the public).* When contamination occurs and symptoms are present, the following steps should be taken to preserve life:

Secure Airway

Avoid all body fluids and protect from secondary contamination of assisting personnel

Be aware of burping and the threat of vomiting to avoid secondary contamination of assisting personnel

Supplement oxygen as indicated while recording and monitoring vitals

Obtain the medical history of the patient to provide further assistance by discovering; the method of decontamination, chemical agents used, duration of exposure, quantity and concentration of chemical agent, patient symptoms, medical history and allergies

Chemical Warfare Survival – Attack and Response

If you have taken the proper steps in prepping taught by our guides you should have a BOB, BOL *(Bug Out Location)* and full body HAZMAT protection adequately prepared. At the onset of a chemical agent attack, immediately apply your preparedness plan and vacate the affected area. If your BOL has been compromised, use the knowledge you've learned from our guides to identify a secondary BOL *(you should have one regardless).* Note: disregard what public officials are advising, vacate the area immediately.

If bugging out is not an option and you are in a building; immediately secure all windows, vents, doors and all other POEs *(point of entry).* All POEs should be sealed with industrial-grade plastic sheeting and duct tape, in addition to turning off your air-conditioner/heater. This is not an ideal situation by any means, and it is highly advised against. If you haven't taken basic survival steps outlined in our guides, you most likely don't have much water or food stored and you could be stuck without for an indefinite amount of time.

If the attack occurs outside when you are away from your BOB, and required items; immediately find adequate shelter to avoid contamination. At which time you will need to follow the steps listed above in securing the building from outside contaminants.

If you're not near a building when an attack occurs *(unlikely, most attacks are likely to occur near urban centers and towns);* attempt to determine wind direction and quickly move cross-wind. Moving downwind or up wind will put you at a greater risk of contamination. If the chemical agents are disbursed over a few hundred square miles, your direction of travel is moot, find the closest shelter regardless of wind direction.

If you're mobile during the attack *(most preppers keep a secondary BOB in their vehicles and you should too);* immediately seek adequate shelter. If you're mobile and have a long-term preparedness plan that consists of bugging out but requires returning to your home for certain supplies; immediately apply your gas mask and continue with your plans. However, practice strict operational awareness; will returning home to fulfill your preparedness plan's requirements put you at risk? If so, make the sacrifice and bug out immediately to your BOL.

When bugging out during a chemical attack and seeking a BOL, you must identify a safe location that should have a high elevation. Bugging out to a BOL with a higher elevation is required due to the weight of aerosol based chemical agents; they are heavier than air and settle downwards.

Stay away from tap water if you are bugging in! The water could be contaminated which is one of the primary reasons most preppers store at least two years' worth of water.

Stay in the loop. Keep lines of communication open when available via HAM radio and hand crank/solar/battery powered radios that are specifically for emergencies with the proper frequencies pre-programmed. You can find this equipment at any survival and outdoor store for a few dollars.

If you have a young infant, there are units that completely enclose the child to prevent contamination available online through sites like Amazon. If such a unit is not available, hold a wet cloth over their mouth and nose *(make sure you are monitoring their breathing in this instance).*

Trust no one; believe it when you see it. If they are not in your trusted network, be extremely cautious and practice standard OpSec *(Operational Security).*

Note: the response steps listed above are for aerosol based attacks such as anthrax, neurotoxins and etc. This type of attack is more likely and should be prioritized. If the water system is contaminated with a liquid contaminant, and you're not a full-on prepper who uses an independent water source, you're already screwed.

MILITIA OPS

This primer has been strictly developed for the use of usCrow Militia Regional Commands, should you choose to join CMF you must enlist with usCrow. Otherwise, you'll do more damage than good to our cause. First and foremost we must clarify that militias are constitutionally sanctioned organizations, unlike the National Guard militias are communities of highly trained civilians and retired/active military personnel, performing basic training and field operations for the means of homeland defense.

Even though enlistment efforts are coordinated by CENTCOM, usCrow still encourages all members to aggressively recruit quality candidates that adhere to our strict Code of Conduct and meet the disqualifications checklist. Should you find a likely candidate online or in person feel free to send them to the usCrow Enlistment Page.

CROW CMF – Oath to the Militia

After gauging your militia prospects and deeming them adequate for service, each enlistment must swear an Oath to the CMF Militia. While symbolic at its core, we still believe a man's word is his bond. Before training begins ensure your enlistment or group of enlistments swear their oaths with a witness present.

I ________________________, do solemnly swear under God that I will commit my life to the protection of my Country and the United States Constitution; protecting Americans of all races and creeds from foreign and domestic attacks. With this oath I will:

Follow the orders of my commanders when those orders do not violate the usCrow Code of Conduct and ethical guidelines

Never divulge the militia's classified activities under any circumstances

Keep the identities of RU/ADC soldiers secret at all costs.

Be an ally to the community, assisting the helpless when natural disasters strike.

Never perform any actions that would embarrass or damage the CROWCMF

OPSEC

Operational security will minimize unforeseen consequences that could inevitably lead to your unit failing its primary objective. Using word of mouth, steganography and cryptography are the best practices when communicating operational guidelines that obtain sensitive materials. When discussing operations over unsecured lines; avoid using full names, dates, times and locations. Family members who are not in your unit should be kept on a 'need to know' basis for their own safety.

Operational security should be enforced by all members and should not be tolerated by Regional Commanders and Commanding Officers. Reprimands should be issued while taking certain situations into account. Long story short; do not openly discuss your activities regardless of their level of security.

CMF Militia PT

PT *(physical training)* for combat soldiers can be tough, so when evaluating your candidates you must ensure they meet minimum physical requirements. Your job as a regional commander is to mold individuals with little to no prior experience into lean machines who do not solely rely on their weaponry. You must first toughen their bodies; within two to three weeks of initial PT, candidates will feel incredibly sore. Allow for a week of recovery, at which time their cardiovascular circulation, metabolism and endurance will slowly increase. To commit your unit to the CMF Militia PT use the Army Issued Pocket PT Guide to outline your PT Program.

Required Equipment

All CMF Militia Members should have the following basic equipment items. Ideally, candidates should have two of each but with the current state of the economy it is not required. If you can't afford the items listed you can also go to local used G.I. Surplus Stores, Swap meets and Yard sales.

I. Combat Boots
II. Combat Gloves *(leather with wool liners)*
III. Combat Fatigues according to your environment
IV. Field Jacket and Liner
V. Ballistics Plate Vest or Bulletproof Vest
VI. Kevlar Helmet
VII. Belt/Leg Rigs/Magazine Attachments
VIII. Camouflage *(paint, veil, mask, shoe polish and etc.)*
IX. Entrenching Tool/Folding Shovel
X. Bug Out Bag *(Containing other required items)*
XI. Gas Mask NATO Israeli Issued
XII. Rifle/Shotgun/Sidearm
XIII. Assault Rope
XIV. Patch to identify the recruit as a US citizen
XV. Patch to identify the member as a usCrow CMF

Field Exercise Equipment Guidelines

When you are in the field you must keep your load as light as possible, so when making your purchases ensure you pay attention to the overall weight of your gear. During drills, weight can make the difference between a successful hump and a 'blue card' situation. Always stock required medication and required dietary items.

Militia BCT Basic Combat Training

Commanders must acquire adequate privately owned property *(written consent required if not owned by the regional commander)* to perform BCT. Recruits should be adequately equipped with the items listed above during BCT. The militia relies on civilian enlistments; therefor training schedules should take into consideration each recruit's individual needs. Recruits who are unable to commit to weekend BCT are not disqualified from the militia, but fellow recruits should assist with their training when available. All CMF Militia Commanders have military experience and are very familiar with BCT, using this knowledge you must outline weekend BCT to include:

Physical Training PT while enforcing disciplinary measures to reinforce obedience to the chain of command. Assisting in the development of an acute attention to detail and common responsibility among the unit

GFT *(ground fighting techniques)* hand to hand combat training, map reading, land navigation, and compass use. These skills should be put to the test during field exercises.

Deadweight and/or 'Pugil Stick' training to simulate carrying an unconscious or immobile body, physical problem solving *(carrying equipment from point A to point B)* outlining specific details and restraints.

Introduction into Marksmanship – Each recruit should be adequately trained by licensed NRA Instructors and/or Military Personnel while providing each recruit with the US Army Rifle Marksmanship M16 & M4 2008 Release

Downrange Marksmanship – The recruit will now fire their weapon they have become familiarized with; firing at various targets, which are progressively further downrange, making each successive target more difficult to hit, with additional pop-up targets at long range

Commanders can simulate proven BCT Primers such as the USMC Survival Course to further enlistments abilities.

Militia Weapons

Mao Tse Tung overthrew the Japanese and Chinese forces with the use of his militia members, Colonial Americans defeated the greatest empire at the time with nothing more than the militia and muskets. The primary fact you must accept for success; if your enemy has it you must have it. Before continuing should you acquire such items you must practice Storing and Caching techniques with strict operational security guidelines. They must be easily accessible but impossible to find. When stocking your legitimate armory you should consider the following:

Accessibility of replacement parts

I. Does it shoot US/Police rounds and do you have re-loaders capable of making these rounds

II. When investing in your arsenal purchase 223/ 5.56/7.62 NATO rounds *(recruits should contribute ammunition as much as possible, without effecting their individual financial obligations)*
III. Other firearms and ammunition to be stored should be 9mm and 12 gauge

Common Militia Firearms

When possible, train with SKS, AK47, 995, M-16, SCAR and AR-15 rifles. Familiarize your candidates with proper shooting techniques such as; Carbine Rifle Tactical Use, Active Shooter Mobile, AK47 Controlled Use, AR-15 / M-16 Armorer. Marksmanship will be further explained throughout this primer.

Militia Explosives

Thermite is a fuel-oxidizer mixture that is used to generate tremendous heat, the mixture of powdered iron oxide/rust and aluminum when ignited will create a reaction producing an approximate 2000 degrees of heat. This makes thermite an excellent tool for the militia. There are no special requirements to make thermite, the mixture is simple 50/50 by weight and can be made in bulk. Thermite can be used in powder form with intake manifolds and 2 inch diameter pipes with a ¼ pound 50/50 mixture. Also see How to make Tannerite.

Strategy and Tactics

I. When training enlistments you should practice some basic fundamentals in guerrilla and insurgent warfare by subjecting the candidates to live action drills using the following techniques:
II. When your enemy advances, retreat unless in an advantageous position that will allow you to defeat your aggressors
III. When the enemy camps *(noticed by a lack of movement and hostile fire)* you then advance and agitate your aggressor with suppression fire, masking targets being eliminated by sniper units
IV. When the enemy tires, hit them with everything you have when the situation allows an offensive action with limited loss of life

V. Know your enemy by becoming familiar with their branches of military and police personnel, movements and SOP *(standard operating procedures)*
VI. Attack the enemy at its weak points
VII. Assign COMM Officers with degrees in Telecom to infiltrate their communication systems.
VIII. Record response times and methodology of attack
IX. Strike at times when an attack is not expected
X. Train militia members to protect Power Stations, Water Plants, and other domestic resources.. be prepared for them to disable our services

LFX – Live Fire Exercises

For the militia unit to have a successful mission objective, the commander must know the unit's abilities and capabilities of its firearms. Officers should have biweekly to monthly LFX, simulating wartime conditions while applying military philosophy/SOP to include but not limited to; LFX concepts, strategies, military terminology, signaling, increasing sustainable training strategies. However, military members and veterans should apply the current experience they have and develop training agendas that fit your unit's needs. The goal for your training maneuvers and LFX should promote combat readiness by implementing:

Establishing a commanding maneuver area or kill box where the unit leader can coordinate troop direction of fire and maneuvering based on METT-T *(Mission, Enemy, Terrain, Troops, and Time)*

A sound integration of organic/non-organic *(direct/indirect)* weapon systems and personnel

Using realistic targets *(such as Tannerite targets, spring loaded targets, etc.)* and return fire *(at a preliminary level a MILES system will not be available, simulation return fire will have to be conducted by automated blank firing systems developed by volunteer mechanical engineers)*

Combat related activities that simulate casualty collection, evacuation, combat and service support

Safety is the first priority during LFX, each exercise must be; reviewed by commanders and engineers assuring no rounds exit the LFX area, and firing exchange meets the highest safety standards

Militia Rifle Marksmanship

The key to successful LFX and training exercises relies on the commander's ability to train and plan for assigned systems and possible contingencies. Collective marksmanship training begins in BCT, while LFX consists of six primary stages that include; range determination, mobile marksmanship, supporting/suppression fire, command and control of movement and fire distribution, integrated firing, static marksmanship for defense and ambush maneuvers, mobile marksmanship for attacking and withdrawing, weapons maintenance and zero calibration. LFX should go in the following order:

I. Individual – Zero weapon, qualify weapon, familiarize with explosive ordinance while engaging the enemy with multiple systems; conducting mobile marksmanship and focusing on IMT
II. Crew – Qualify with crew-served weapon if applicable while engaging enemy with multiple systems, rehearse during LFX
III. Buddy – Engage enemies with multiple systems during LFX
IV. Fire Team – Coordinated movement exercise, IMT and communication using arm-and-hand signals should be perfected during dry fire LFX.
V. Squad – The LFX combines the platoon introducing maneuvers, command and control process *(fire team and squad leaders)* complicating of the exercise. Force-on-force training to precede all LFX and higher.
VI. Company and Larger Units – Before any training is conducted that expends blank or live ammunition, a dry-fire or walk-through exercise should be conducted. This allows the unit to improve movement techniques, command and control, safety, and many other areas before critical resources are used. Due to OPSEC we usCrow can't publicly outline this exercise, however regional commanders should be well aware of the requirements during company and large unit LFX.

The simplicity of these firearms means that they can be disguised as or concealed within umbrellas, canes, pens, tire-pressure gauges etc., creating very effective weapons of surprise and assassination. Plan ahead, if you own an Ammunition Reloader such as the RCBS Rock Chucker Reloader you will be better positioned to barter and defend.

Slap 12 Gauge - Zip Gun

This is the simplest zip gun design; parts are cheap, readily available and can be assembled in less than an hour. It can be fired and reloaded several times a minute and has a moderate kick. Loaded, it weighs about 2-1/4 pounds. Basic cost is under $5.00. It is made of common, galvanized plumbing pipe, obtained from a hardware store, plumbing supply store or even junkyard.

Materials Required:

- 1″ Pipe 6″ in length, threaded on one end.
- 1″ Pipe-cap
- 3/4″ Pipe 10″ in length.
- 1″ Dowel
- No. 16 nail
- 1-1/8″ Circle of thin cardboard

First try to insert the 3/4″ pipe into the 1″ pipe. It must slide through every time with no sticking or slowing. Make a reamer from 7″ or 8″ of your 1″ dowel. Cut a piece 5 x 3-1/16″ from a sheet of emery cloth, wrap it around the dowel and glue it in place.

When you buy your dowel take the 1″ pipe and make sure the dowel goes in with some space to spare. If the dowel fits exactly, it's too big and you'll have to choose the next size down.

Use the reamer to enlarge the inside of the 1″ pipe. Move it in and out of the 1″ pipe along the sides a few times to get rid of any burrs or uneven areas. Try the 3/4″ pipe again and if it won't fall through without slowing, do it again until it will. Go over the outside of the 3/4″ pipe, a few times with the emery cloth.

Next make the hammer. First cut a 1/2″ piece of the dowel. Choose a drill the same width as the No. 16 nail and drill a hole through the exact center of the dowel piece. With a hacksaw, cut the nail 5/8 of an inch past the head. Then cut a 1-1/8″ wide circle of thin cardboard and with the nail point, punch a hole in its middle. Push the nail section through the dowel hole and push the cardboard over its end with the rough side on top. Next push the hammer unit into the cap, cardboard side up. The cardboard is to keep the dowel and hammer in the cap. In order to disassemble, just pick the hammer unit out by the nail.

Screw the cap on, put a 12 gauge shell in the 3/4″ pipe, put the 3/4″ pipe in the 1″ pipe and it's ready to fire. Hold the 1″ end-cap in the right hand and with the left hand slam the 3/4″ pipe backwards to fire. Pull the 3/4″ pipe out to reload.

This weapon can be improved by using a machine screw, nut and washer as the hammer assembly. Sharpen the machine screw to a shallow point and push it through the end cap then fasten it on the inside of the cap with the nut and washer. Cut a thumb groove it the rim of the 3/4″ pipe to allow spent shells to be pulled out with the thumbnail.

Don't be tempted to fire 3″ or 3-1/2″ magnum loads in this weapon. For safety's sake stick with the 2-3/4″ shells, the extra power of the magnums is just wasted in a weapon with a short barrel and no chamber anyway. This weapon is reliable only at very close range.

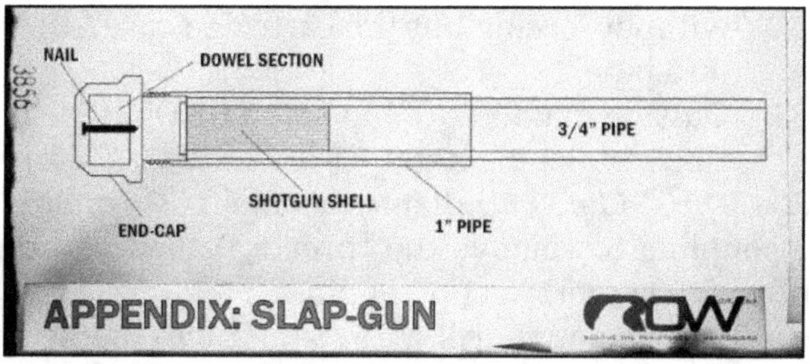

Improvised 9mm (or .38 caliber) Pipe Pistol

A very simple 9 mm pistol can be made from 1/4" steel gas or water pipe and fittings. These plans can be modified to allow the use of just about any handgun or shotgun cartridge. I would discourage the use of very powerful loading such as the .44 magnum, .357 magnum or 12 gauge 3 1/2" magnum shells in these weapons.

Materials Required:

- 1/4" nominal size steel pipe 4 to 6 inches long with threaded ends.
- 1/4" Solid pipe plug
- Two (2) steel pipe couplings
- Metal strap – roughly 1/8" x 1/4" x 5"
- Two (2) elastic bands
- Flat head nail – 6D or 8D *(approx. 1/16" diameter)*
- Two (2) wood screws #8
- Wood 8" x 5" x 1"
- Drill
- 1/4" wood or metal rod, *(approx. 8" long)*

Procedure:

1. Carefully inspect pipe and fittings.
    1. Make sure that there are NO cracks or other flaws in the pipe or fittings.
    2. Check inside diameter of pipe using a 9 mm cartridge as a gauge. The bullet should closely fit into the pipe

without forcing but the cartridge case SHOULD NOT fit into pipe.

   3. Outside diameter of pipe MUST NOT BE less than 1 1/2 times bullet diameter *(.536 inches; 1.37 cm)*

2. Drill a 9/16" *(1.43 cm)* diameter hole 3/8" *(approx. 1 cm)* into one coupling to remove the thread. Drilled section should fit tightly over smooth section of pipe.
3. For a 9mm weapon, drill a 25/64" *(1 cm)* diameter hole 3/4" *(1.9 cm)* into pipe. Use cartridge as a gauge; when a cartridge is inserted into the pipe, the base of the case should be even with the end of the pipe. The barrel is now chambered for 9mmThread coupling tightly onto pipe, drilled end first.
4. For a .38 caliber weapon, drill a 25/64" *(1 cm)* diameter hole 1-1/8" *(2.86 cm)* into pipe. Use cartridge as a gauge; when a cartridge is inserted into the pipe, the shoulder of the case should butt against the end of the pipe. The barrel is now chambered for .38. Thread coupling tightly onto pipe, drilled end first.
5. Drill a hole in the center of the pipe plug just large enough for the nail to fit through. Hole MUST be centered in plug.
6. Push nail through plug until head of nail is flush with square end. Cut nail off at other end 1/16" *(.158 cm)* away from plug. Round off end of nail with file.
7. Bend metal strap to "U" shape and drill holes for wood screws. File two small notches at top.
8. Saw or otherwise shape 1" *(2.54 cm)* thick hard wood into stock.
9. Drill a 9/16" diameter *(1.43 cm)* hole through the stock. The center of the hole should be approximately 1/2" *(1.27 cm)* from the top.
10. Slide the pipe through this hole and attach front coupling. Screw drilled plug into rear coupling. *NOTE: IF 9/16" DRILL IS NOT AVAILABLE CUT A "V" GROOVE IN THE TOP OF THE STOCK AND TAPE PIPE SECURELY IN PLACE.*
11. Position metal strap on stock so that top will hit the head of the nail. Attach to stock with wood screw on each side.
12. String elastic bands from front coupling to notch on each side of the strap.

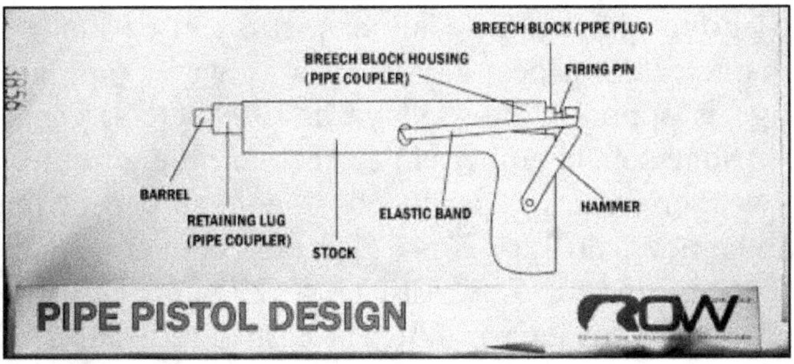

Test Fire This Weapon before Hand Firing;

1. Locate a barrier such as a stone wall or large tree which you can stand behind in case the pistol ruptures when fired.
2. Mount pistol solidly to a table or other rigid support at least ten feet in front of the barrier.
3. Attach a cord to the firing strap on the pistol.
4. Holding the other end of the cord, go behind the barrier.
5. Pull the cord so that the firing strap is held back.
6. Release the cord to fire the pistol. *(If pistol does not fire, shorten the elastic bands or increase their number.)* Important: Fire at least five rounds from behind the barrier and then re-inspect the pistol before you attempt to hand fire it.

Pistol Operation:

1. To Load:
    1. Remove plug from rear coupling.
    2. Place cartridge into pipe.
    3. Replace plug making sure it is seated against rear of cartridge case.
2. To Fire:
    1. Pull strap back and hold with thumb until ready.
    2. Release strap to fire.
3. To Remove Shell Case:
    1. Remove plug from rear coupling.
    2. Insert 1/4″ diameter steel or wooden rod into front of pistol and push shell case out.

22 LR or .22 short Improvised Pipe Pistol

Using the above plans a .22 Caliber pistol can be made from 1/8″ nominal diameter extra heavy, steel gas or water pipe and fittings. Lethal range is approximately 33 yards (30 meters). This is also a rimmed cartridge so a chamber isn't necessary but a tighter and more powerful weapon will be produced if a chamber is reamed. To produce a chamber, drill a 15/64″ (1/2 cm) diameter hole 9/16″ (1-1/2 cm) deep in pipe for a .22 LR. (If a .22 short cartridge is used, drill hole 3/8″ (1 cm) deep). When a cartridge is inserted into the pipe, the shoulder of the case should butt against the end of the pipe. The firing pin hole must be drilled off center because this is a rim-fire weapon. Also the firing pin should be filed like a slot or flat-head screwdriver with two flat surfaces opposite each other converging in a rounded point. This will provide more positive function. Spent cartridges will become jammed so a 1/8″ wooden dowel will be required to force them out before reloading.

Materials Required:

- Steel pipe, extra heavy, 1/8″ (3 mm) nominal diameter and 6″ (15 cm) long with threaded ends (nipple)
- Solid pipe plug, 1/8″ (3 mm) nominal diameter
- 2 steel pipe couplings, 1/8″ (3 mm) nominal diameter
- Metal strap, approximately 1/8″ x 1/4″ x 5″ (3 mm x 6 mm x 125 mm or 12-1/2 cm)
- Elastic bands
- Flat head nail – 6D or 8D (approximately 1/16″ (1-1/2 mm) diameter
- 2 wood screws, #8
- Hard wood, 8″ x 5″ x 1″ (20 cm x 12-1/2 cm x 2-1/2 cm)
- Drill
- Wood or metal rod, 1/8″ (3 mm) diameter and 8″ (20 cm) long
- Saw or knife

NATO Carbine 7.62mm

A rifle caliber weapon can be made from water or gas pipe and fittings. Standard NATO 7.62mm (.308) cartridges are used for ammunition. Great caution must be used with this weapon and I must be honest and admit that I have not even attempted to make a weapon which fires high-powered rifle ammunition out of water or gas pipes and fittings. I would recommend acquiring a 20″ length of seamless (DOM) steel tubing to fabricate the barrel for this weapon. A steel supplier will have this type of tubing but be sure to ask for DOM (drawn over mandrel) seamless tubing. Be sure it's a good quality steel for this type of use. Ask for 4140 or 4130 steel. If you are questioned as to what the tubing is to be used for you should respond that you are replacing a part for a high-pressure boiler or hydraulic system. A standard pipe-die can be used to cut the threading on one end of the barrel. If you are unable to obtain seamless tubing then you should get a 20″ length of water pipe, the ¼" barrel pipe should fit inside this pipe and epoxy can be used to fasten it within the larger pipe. This will double the strength of the barrel. Make sure to leave enough of the threading on the ¼" pipe exposed to allow it to be mated securely with the coupler.

Materials Required:

- Wood approximately 2″ x 4″ x 30″
- 1/4″ nominal size iron water or gas pipe 20″ long threaded at one end.
- 3/8″ to 1/4 reducer
- 3/8″ x 1-1/2″ threaded pipe
- 3/8″ pipe coupling
- Metal strap approximately 1/2″ x 1/16″ x 4″.
- Twine, heavy (100 yards approx.) and Shellac or duct tape or metal strapping and screws
- 3 wood screws and screwdriver
- Flat head nail about 1″ long
- Hand drill
- Saw or knife
- File
- Pipe wrench
- Elastic bands
- Solid 3/8″ pipe plug

Procedure:

1. Inspect pipe and fittings carefully.

    1. Be sure that there are NO cracks or flaws.
    2. Check inside diameter of pipe. A 7.62 mm projectile should fit into 3/8″ pipe.
2. Cut stock from wood using saw or knife.
3. Cut a 1/4″ deep "V" groove in top of the stock.
4. Fabricate rifle barrel from pipe.
    1. File or drill inside diameter of threaded end of 20″ pipe for about 1/4″ so neck of cartridge case will fit in.
    2. Screw reducer onto threaded pipe using pipe wrench.
    3. Screw short threaded pipe into reducer.
    4. Turn 3/8 pipe coupling onto threaded pipe using pipe wrench. All fittings should be as tight as possible. Do not split fittings.
5. Coat pipe and "V" groove of stock with shellac or lacquer. While still wet, place pipe in "V" groove and wrap pipe and stock together using two layers of twine. Coat twine with shellac or lacquer after each layer. Duct tape or metal strapping secured with wood screws can also be used to fasten the barrel to the stock.
6. Drill a hole through center of pipe plug large enough for nail to pass through.
7. File threaded end of plug flat.
8. Push nail through plug and out of threaded end 1/32″ (2 mm) past the plug.
9. Screw plug into coupling.
10. Bend 4″ metal strap into "L" shape and drill hole for wood screw. Notch metal strap on the long side 1/2″ from bend.
11. Position metal strap on stock so that top will hit the head of the nail. Attach to stock with wood screw.
12. Place screw in each side of stock about 4″ in front of metal strap. Pass elastic bands through notch in metal strap and attach to screw on each side of the stock.

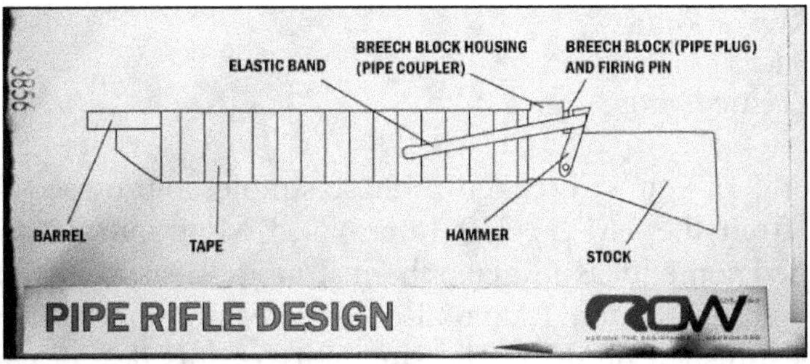

Simple Improvised 12 gauge Shotgun

A 12-gauge shotgun can be made with the above plans from 3/4″ water or gas pipe and fittings. It will not be necessary to bore a chamber in this weapon because the 12 gauge shell is a rimmed cartridge and the rim will shoulder up against the end of the pipe. The firing pin hole should be drilled dead center in the plug and the firing pin should be made from a larger nail, up to about 1/8″. This weapon can be built as a pistol with a short barrel or with a long barrel (around 20″ or so) and a full length stock. In the latter case the weapon can be fastened to the stock with metal strapping and screws or even with duct tape. Don't be tempted to experiment with any magnum loads in this weapon, just stick with standard 2 ¾" shells. You will need some sort of stick or dowel to force spent shells out of this weapon as they tend to become quite jammed in the chamber after firing.

Materials Required:

- Wood 2″ x 4″ x 32″
- 3/4″ nominal size water or gas pipe 20″ to 30″ long threaded on one end.
- 3/4″ steel coupling
- Solid 3/4″ pipe plug
- Metal strap (1/4″ x 1/16″ x 4″)
- Duct tape or metal strapping and screws
- 3 wood screws and screwdriver
- Flat head nail 6D or 8D
- Hand drill

- Saw or knife
- File
- Elastic Bands

Note: Some of you will recognize these simple, improvised firearms, designs from the FM 31-210 Improvised Munitions Handbook. I have added some ideas to make the instructions easier to follow and the final product safer. I have also provided some drawings which detail the finished product. The simplicity of this design was likely the key factor in its being included in the FM 31-210; however it has some serious drawbacks. It is very dangerous in that it is prone to accidental discharge upon dropping or other impact. It has no safety and the firing pin is held in place with only the forward pressure of the elastic upon the hammer. If the pipe plug is not tightened down far enough the backward movement of the fired cartridge could push and eject the firing pin at high speed into the shooter's eye. The potential for injury increases further with the possibility of a ruptured primer. This occurs when the firing pin pierces the primer allowing the propellant gasses the vent out of the back of the cartridge; in the case of this firearm design a ruptured primer would force the firing pin out at very high speed into the face of the shooter. With caution these risks can be reduced. Remember these precautions;

- Always be sure the pipe plug is tightened until it contacts the back of the cartridge when loading, allowing no room for backward movement of the cartridge.
- Be sure that the elastic tension upon the hammer is not too excessive, just enough to reliably fire the weapon.
- Be sure that the firing pin is not sharpened or too long as this can cause rupture of the primer.
- Don't carry or store these weapons loaded unless absolutely necessary.

Match Gun

An improvised firearm can be built using safety match heads as the propellant and a metal object as the projectile. Lethal range is about

40 yards (36 meters). This weapon is very simple to construct and is well suited for use as a booby trap.

Materials Required

- Metal pipe 24″ (61 cm) long and 3/8″ (1 cm) in diameter (nominal size) or its equivalent, threaded on one end.
- End cap to fit pipe
- Safety matches – 3 books of 20 matches each.
- Wood – 28″ x 4″ x 1″ (70 cm x 10 cm x 2.5 cm)
- Safety fuse OR "Strike-anywhere matches" (2)
- Electrical tape or string
- Metal strap, about 4″ x 12″ and 1″ x 3/16″ (10 cm x 6 mm x 4.5 cm)
- 2 rags, about 1″ x 12″ and 1″ x 3″ (2-1/2 cm x 30 cm and 2-1/2 cm x 8 cm)
- Wood screws
- Metal object (steel rod, bolt with head cut off, etc.), approximately 7/16″(11 mm) in diameter, and 7/16″ (11 mm) long if iron or steel, 1-1/4″ (31 mm) long if aluminum, 5/16″ (8 mm) long if lead. A large ball bearing, of the appropriate size, will fly straighter than a cylindrical object.
- Metal disk 1″ (2-1/2 cm) in diameter and 1/16″ (1-1/2 mm) thick
- Bolt, 3/32″ (2-1/2 mm) or smaller in diameter and nut to fit
- Saw or knife

Procedure

1. Carefully inspect pipe and fittings. Be sure that there are NO cracks or other flaws.
2. Drill small hole in center of end cap. If safety fuse is used, be sure it will pass through this hole.
3. Cut stock from wood using saw or knife.
4. Cut 3/8″ (9-1/2 mm) deep "V" groove in top of stock.
5. Screw end cap onto pipe until finger tight.
6. Attach pipe to stock with string or tape.
7. Bend metal strap into "L" shape and drill holes for wood screw. Notch metal on long side 1/2″ (1 cm) from bend.

8. Position metal strap on stock so that the top will hit the center of hole drilled in end cap.
9. Attach metal disk to strap with nut and bolt. This will deflect blast from hole in end cap when gun is fired. Be sure that head of bolt is centered on hole in end cap.
10. Attach strap to stock with wood screws.
11. Place screw on each side of stock about 4″ (10 cm) in front of metal strap. Pass elastic bands through notch in metal strap and attach to screw on each side of stock.

Operation

1. Cut off match heads from 3 books of matches with knife. Pour match heads into pipe.
2. Fold one end of 1″ x 12″ rag 3 times so that it becomes a 1″ square of 3 thicknesses. Place rag into pipe to cover match heads, folded end first. Tamp firmly WITH CAUTION.
3. Place metal object into pipe. Place 1″ x 3″ rag into pipe to cover projectile. Tamp firmly WITH CAUTION.
4. Carefully cut off tips of heads of 2 "strike-anywhere" matches with knife.
5. Place one tip in hole in end cap. Push in with wooden match stick.
6. Place second match tip on a piece of tape. Place tape so match tip is directly over hole in end cap.
7. When ready to fire, pull metal strap back and release.

When safety fuse is available:

1. Remove end cap from pipe. Knot one end of safety fuse. Thread safety fuse through hole in end cap so that knot is on inside of end cap.
2. Follow steps 1 through 3 above.
3. Tie several matches to safety fuse near outside of end cap. NOTE: Bare end of safety fuse should be inside match head cluster.
4. Wrap match covers around matches and tie. Striker should be in contact with match bands.
5. Replace end cap on pipe.

6. When ready to fire, pull match cover off with strong, firm, quick motion.

PRACTICE SAFETY AT ALL TIMES!

CAMOUFLAGE

A "Ghillie" is a Scottish game-keeper. *Pronounce the word "Gee' lee", starting with the glutteral gee (guh), not a jay sound (jee).* These guys found that they could sew strips of burlap to their clothes, and then wait patiently for poachers to come by — as long as they remained still, their game would nearly step on them.

In most lighting conditions, detection is a result of both brightness and shape contrasts with the background. Most camouflage fatigues do a pretty good job of matching the general brightness level of foliage, desert, etc. The camouflage pattern printed onto the material attempts to match the shapes inherent in the background as well. Unfortunately, all camouflage fatigues follow the human form pretty closely — resulting in an overall shape that looks like a human, not natural background. The problem lies in the fact that the fatigues are trying to duplicate a three-dimensional pattern of shapes *(foliage, usually)* with a two-dimensional camouflage pattern applied to a sheet of fabric. In most lighting conditions, it don't work very well. Now, camouflage fatigues and jackets and such certainly blend in much better than blue jeans and T-shirts, but they aren't totally effective — and cannot be without adding three-dimensional noise to the essentially two-dimensional form of a human.

A Ghillie Suit is a very effective camouflage technique that uses strips of material to break up the outline of the wearer. This fools the eye of the enemy — the brain sees no recognizable shapes. By adding strips of burlap, or camouflage netting, or branches off bushes to your clothing, you create the three-dimensional pattern disruption I was talking about above. The advantage comes from creating patches that are nearly the same color as the environment, while simultaneously creating ultra-dark shadows alongside. Printed fabric cannot create black patches as dark as real shadows the shadow is about 2 orders of magnitude darker than the darkest printed black fabric.

Step by Step Instructions

I. Obtain an old pair of coveralls — this is called the foundation of the suit. In a pinch a fatigue blouse and pants will suffice.
II. Get some burlap from your local fabric store *(about 4 yards).* The more burlap you use the more effective *(up to a point) will* be the Ghillie Suit — however, it will rapidly become heavy *(Army and Marine sniper suits weigh up to 20 pounds or more).*
III. Dye the burlap some dark to medium green *(Rit dye — try to match foliage greens).* Instructions are on the dye package, Dye a little *(half a yard)* brown *(use sparingly).*
IV. Cut the burlap into strips 2-3″ wide and anywhere from 6″ to 12″ long *(mix up the widths and lengths)*
V. Sew one end of each strip to the outside of your foundation — all over it. Space them so that the ends of the upper strips will overlap the attachment points of strips lower down. The sides do not need to overlap. Fill in by tying vines, small foliate branches, grass, etc. to the suit by knotting the strips around it, or sew strings or cord at random over the suit to tie these materials in.

Crawl and enjoy!

Tactical Advantage of a Ghillie Suit

Ghillie Suits are used for stealth — move as slowly as possible, if at all. If one hides in bushes, and uses single shots, the enemy won't be able to find you unless they are looking almost directly at you when you fire. Be careful that muzzle blast doesn't disturb foliage or raise dust.

An effective technique is to hide in the base of bushes near a path, let the enemy go past, while picking them off with single shots from the rear. A gun cover can be made using the same techniques and should be used to disrupt the shape of the weapon.

Other habitat based Ghillie Suits can be built in the same manner for tundra, winter and arctic, tropical, desert, forest and much more. Simply use the same process matching the coloring of the environment you are in.

HOMEMADE EXPLOSIVES

When the SHTF, there will be mayhem and mass hysteria, making a healthy repertoire of homemade explosives a worthy addition to your post disaster arsenal. However, we highly stress this information is not to be used until AFTER the shit hits the fan. Failure to comply will land you some serious charges with a considerable amount of jail time, not to mention the possibility of harm to yourself and others. This guide outlines basic mixtures of simple household items that can cause substantial damage in a variety of uses; disabling vehicles, clearing rooms, diversions and etc.

Molotov Cocktail

Molotov cocktails are one of the most well-known homemade explosives across the world. Known for their simplicity, Molotov cocktails can be made from various and common ingredients. Typically these can be used as an RCA *(riot control agent),* structure demolition, and many other diverse uses. The disadvantage of molotovs is their limited range *(the distance you can throw them*) and the burn duration *(relatively low),* and the depletion of resources *(when at risk).*

I. Glass bottle or glass container to shatter upon impact, allowing the ignited accelerate to quickly engulf its target

II. Motor Oil 25% mixed with Gasoline 50%

III. One Styrofoam cup ripped into 1/4in x 1/4in pieces, which is not required for ignition

IV. Use a rag to ignite the accelerate, which can be dipped in gasoline *(not drenched)* enough to create a controlled ignition. Roughly 14in long fuses made of cloth should be wedged tightly through the opening, with 7in inside and 7in outside

V. Light the end of the fuse after you've identified your target and throw it immediately

Pipe bomb

Pipe bombs have been a favorite in the backwoods of Kentucky and the mountains of Colorado, due to their simplicity and a substantial increase in device control. Pipe bombs are extremely illegal and even the materials required to make a pipe bomb are illegal in some states.

Mercury Fulminate

To prepare mercury fulminate in the absence of proper detonating devices;

I. Mix 5gr mercury with 35ml nitric acid.
II. Heat gradually until the solution bubbles and turns green.
III. Pour into a small flask full of ethyl alcohol producing red fumes.
IV. In 30min when red fumes turn white.
V. After 3min slowly add distilled water.
VI. Extract small white crystals which are mercury fulminate, wash the samples several time and test with litmus paper to remove undesirable acid.

Diversionary Smoke Bomb

Smoke bombs are a relative solution of potassium nitrate and sugar, potassium nitrate can be found in hardware stores as a raw material or it can be found in stump remover. Smoke bombs can be used as diversions, provide defensive cover and offensive screens.

I. Pour about 3 parts potassium nitrate KNO3 to 2 parts sugar into the skillet *(5:3 ratio is also good)*. Measurements don't need to be exact, but you want more KNO3 than sugar. For example, you can use 1-1/2 cups KNO3 and 1 cup sugar. If you use equal amounts of KNO3 and sugar, your smoke bomb will be harder to light and will burn more slowly. As you approach the 5:3 KNO3: sugar ratio, you get a smoke bomb that burns more quickly.
II. Apply low heat to the pan. Stir the mixture with a spoon using long strokes. If you see the grains of sugar starting to melt along the edges where you are stirring, remove the pan from the heat and reduce the temperature before continuing.
III. Basically you are caramelizing sugar. The mixture will melt and become a caramel or chocolate color. Continue heating/stirring until the ingredients are liquefied. Remove from heat.
IV. Pour the liquid onto a piece of foil. You can pour a smaller amount onto a separate piece, to test the batch. You can pour the smoke bomb into any shape, onto an object, or into a mold. The shape and size will affect the burning pattern.

V. Allow the smoke bomb to cool, and then you can peel it off the foil.

VI. You can also increase the amount of materials used in equal parts in larger containers and canisters.

EVASION TACTICS

The following steps will outline the necessary precautions and procedures to evade hostile enemy forces in unfamiliar territories during times of conflict. Many of the steps outlined in this primer are SOP (Standard Operating Procedures) taught to military personnel, militia units, and special operators.

One of the fundamentals taught throughout the military is the certainty of failure and the unexpected consequences for miscellaneous variables. When disaster strikes and not everything went according to plan, evasion may be your only option. You will need to immediately vacate the area covering great distances in a relatively short amount of time. Before vacating plan your route of evasion, instead of running away in a random direction. Approximations made in the heat of the moment, as long as they are within reasonable proximity to your goal, will have to suffice. After you have put a safe amount of distance between you and your enemy, rest and regain situational awareness while applying your awareness to your escape plan. You will need to pinpoint your location using a compass, the sun, landmarks, G.P.S., or your map.

To better your chances for your survival we have highlighted crucial skills you will need to escape enemy combatants, including skills taught in Special Forces, Navy Seals, the Marine Corps and etc.

LOCATION ASSESSMENT

If your compass or G.P.S. has become inoperable or grossly inaccurate you will need to apply some basic tricks used for thousands of years to this day. One of the easiest to use is the sunrise, the sun rises from the east, which means north is to your left and south is to your right.

Use your watch as a compass

1. The sun will always 'appear' to be south of the north temperate time zone and north of the south. Watches can be used to get a precise northern direction, thus compensating for the eastern and western movements the sun makes.
2. Hold the watch level with the hour hand pointing directly at the sun
3. Draw an angle in your head with the vertex *(The point about which an angle is measured)* centered on the watch, with one line through noon and the other along the hour hand.
4. Decrease this angle by 50%
5. This new angle formed now projects the precise southern direction

Using the Southern Cross at Night

When you are in the southern hemisphere you can find south by locating what is known as the *'Southern Cross'*. The Southern Cross is a constellation with four bright stars, making it easily identifiable; when these stars are connected they form a cross. Using your mind's eye draw an imaginary line from the bottom of the cross extending 4 1/2 times its length. Draw another line at the end of the length going straight down and you now have your southern reference point.

Using Shadow to find Direction

Drive a straight stake or stick into the ground with at least 3 feet exposed to the sun's rays. Make the tip of the shadow it casts, wait for approximately 15 minutes and make the tip of the shadow's location again. Draw a line from your first marking to your second marking, this method will always point north. Note: In south temperate zones this direction will be south.

EVASION KEY POINTS

Now that we have our general direction adequately plotted, we have to practice basic precautions as we navigate across hostile territory. Simply knowing these steps is not enough to guarantee survival, however it is absolutely necessary you comply with these simple guidelines to better your chances for survival.

Determine your direction, choose a direction with forgiving terrain and less obstacles to navigate, thus avoiding exhaustion. Densely vegetated areas with moderate terrain work particularly well when cover is needed. If a map is available, study the slopes carefully to identify the most convenient and safe exit points.

Check your location and direction often, deviations from a linear direction are guaranteed due to topography and gradual deviation patterns

Rivers and moving bodies of water make excellent directional indicators *(Note: not all rivers flow from South to North).* Rivers are almost always accompanied by towns and are almost guaranteed to be patrolled by hostile forces. If your situation required the use of the river during evasion, attempt to stay out of the open.

If you can acquire a boat for evasion, but your duration of travel calls for intermittent stops, compensate by submerging or camouflaging the boat.

Ridges are typically more exposed but much easier to travel upon. If your situation allows for traveling on ridges and crests, do so while elevating your scouting precautions.

When near hostile enemy location, move after sunset and in the twilight, using the low visibility as cover while maintaining enough visibility to target enemies and equipment. Do not make noise, noise travels a couple hundred yards *(if loud enough)*, will expose your location.

Never sleep near a fire, water supply or enemy locations.

Before approaching your FOB *(Forward Operating Base)* or Camp, investigate the surrounding areas for hostile targets and eliminate. After eliminating your targets and hiding the remains, you will need to evacuate your current compromised camp location.

In dense vegetation insects can be a killer, always use sufficient amount of insect repellant.

Use the environment and surroundings to your advantage, many of the basic essentials you need to survive are most likely present. I.E. Water, Food, Shelter.

WATER GUIDE

The bullet points below describe the amount of water you should be drinking when traveling by foot. This chart does not accommodate for strenuous movement and excess aridity. Anxiety and physical stress always require more water. In addition, wind and sun condition are likely to cause variations.

120 degrees Fahrenheit / 48 degrees Celsius

No Water – 2 Days

1 qt. Water – 2 Days

2 qt. Water – 2 Days

4 qt. Water – 2.5 Days

10 qt. Water – 3 Days

20 qt. Water – 4.5 Days

110 degrees Fahrenheit / 43.3 degrees Celsius

No Water – 3 Days

USCROW

1qt. Water – 3 Days

2 qt. Water – 3.5 Days

4 qt. Water – 4 Days

10 qt. Water – 5 Days

20 qt. Water – 7 Days

90 degrees Fahrenheit / 32.2 degrees Celsius

No Water – 7 Days

1qt. Water – 8 Days

2 qt. Water – 9 Days

4 qt. Water – 10.5 Days

10 qt. Water – 15 Days

20 qt. Water – 23 Days

70 degrees Fahrenheit / 21.1 degrees Celsius

No Water – 10 Days

1 qt. Water – 11 Days

2 qt. Water – 12 Days

4 qt. Water – 14 Days

10 qt. Water – 20.5 Days

20 qt. Water – 32 Days

50 degrees Fahrenheit / 10.0 degrees Celsius

No Water – 10 Days

1qt. Water – 11 Days

2 qt. Water – 12 Days

4 qt. Water – 14.5 Days

10 qt. Water – 21 Days

20 qt. Water – 32 Days

MEDICAL

TRAUMA RESPONSE GUIDELINES

This comprehensive guide will outline the standard medical procedures for first responders, and the steps required treating traumatic injuries. Survival hinges on your ability to properly respond to common injuries and life threatening injuries. With little access to EMT's, nurses and doctors, you're going to have to save your friend or family member's life.

As previously reviewed in our Bug Out Bag Article, an EMT/First Aid Kit is essential. Ensure your kits are properly sterilized and adequately stocked with; bandage scissors *(knife can be used in emergencies),* forceps/mini scalpel, airway kit, compresses, tourniquets, hazmat materials, Mylar blanket, burn dressing, ammonia inhalants, eye pads, bandages and etc.. You can get these bags fully stocked around $50-75.

First Aid Guide Medical Safety Guidelines

Always wash hands thoroughly before and after treatment

Always wear disposable gloves that are puncture free

Properly dispose of contaminated materials in properly labeled red bags (when available)

Never recap used needles

Use only sterilized needles and sharp instruments

Provide peer training when available

SOFT TISSUE INJURIES AND WOUNDS

Soft tissue injuries involve the skin, subcutaneous tissues, and underlying musculature. An injury to these tissues is commonly referred to as a flesh wound. These injuries are usually extremely painful.

Closed Wounds

Inspect for any underlying fractures and splint if fracture is suspected. To secure limbs to a splint; belts, neckerchiefs, rope, or any suitable material may be used. If possible, tie the limb at two places above and two places below the break.

Open Wounds

Expose all wound sites while clearing the wound of any loose foreign material *(shrapnel, dirt, debris and etc.).* Apply dressing and bandages to all open wounds and control bleeding.

Incised Wounds

Edges of the wound may need to be drawn together prior to dressing these wounds by using a sterile needle and thread using that should be included in your first aid kit. When closing wounds there is no 'one right way' other than ensuring your sutures adequately closes the wound.

Impaled Objects

Stabilize the object, if the object impedes transportation to a secondary staging area, careful shortening of the object may be requiring by immobilizing the object. Do not remove the object unless it interferes with CPR or causes a complete airway obstruction.

Evisceration

Cover the evisceration with sterile, saline soaked dressing. Support the evisceration with additional dressings while maintaining warmth.

Gun Shot Wounds

When possible, identify the type of weapon and caliber used. Immediate evacuation to a secondary staging area is typically required. Access the patient's entry and exit wounds. Expose the wound site and treat the injury as per the above listed guideline. Clear the wounds of all foreign and loose material, including ammunition fragments including the bullet itself when proper medical facilities are not available. Control bleeding while considering internal bleeding, fractures, and injuries to underlying organs and structures. Pay close attention to the patient's vitals and be prepared to manage cardiorespiratory distress or arrest.

EXTERNAL AND INTERNAL BLEEDING

Early recognition of blood loss, internal or external, is critical in managing a hemorrhaging patient. This early recognition allows shock to be managed early and aggressively by controlling external bleeding.

Survey the patient while controlling any major bleeding, applying direct pressure using a gloved hand or sterile dressing. Have the patient rest the injured area and elevate the limb affected, when appropriate use pressure points to the wound, if bleeding is not controlled by direct pressure use a tourniquet as a last resort. If bleeding persists apply additional dressing and pressure as needed in layers. Never remove dressings once applied.

Administer high concentration oxygen by non-re-breathe mask and assist ventilation as required. If shock is present treat accordingly. Survey the area again and assess the distal color, warmth, circulation and movement prior to application of dressings and bandages, and reassess after applying bandages. Examine all wounds for penetrating or impaled objects, prior to applying direct pressure and dressings remove all loose surface material.

If a dressing becomes blood soaked, apply additional dressings over the original dressing. Secure all dressing appropriately so they do not slip while maintaining pressure on the wound site. Reassess.

Internal Bleeding

Minimize patient movement and suspect underlying fractures, internal injuries. If no surgical staff is present and no one is capable of performing the operation the patient will die in a short amount of time.

Bleeding from Orifices

Apply loose dressings externally to absorb blood and prevent infection; do not pack the orifice with dressings. Seek immediate help from medical staff.

Use of a Tourniquet

Application of a tourniquet should be used as a last resort to control bleeding. The tourniquet should be made from wide material such as 7-10cm *(3-4in)* wide cravat or blood pressure cuff. Prior to application distal circulatory and neurological status must be assessed. Tourniquets should be applied as close to the injury as possible and if the injury is below the knee, the tourniquet must be applied above just tight enough to stop the bleeding. If a blood pressure cuff is use it should be inflated to 30mm Hg above systolic. Tourniquets may be released after two hours if bleeding discontinues.

Amputations

Amputations are extremely traumatic and can focus all of the treatment to one injury, while other life threatening injuries and illnesses could be present. Amputations are emotionally difficult to deal with for the patient and those involved.

Shock will almost certainly need to be treated. The use of tourniquets can be implemented above joints and any anesthetics available may be used. If no further medical help is available the wound must be cauterized immediately after application of the tourniquet and after the area has been cleaned. Locate all of the severed parts and rinse gently with sterile saline to remove loose debris and gross contamination *(do not scrub).* Wrap the severed parts in sterile saline soaked dressings and inside a labeled plastic bag. Place the bag in a container that has been filled with ice and water.

FRACTURES AND DISLOCATIONS

Plaster of Paris *(Newspapers, Water, and Thickening Agent)* is one of the most common methods used to immobilize a limb. This cast is made from a preparation of gypsum that sets hard when water is added. Operation procedures depend on the location and severity of the fracture, for example:

Closed or simple fractures - the two ends of the broken bone are lined up and held in place. The limb is thoroughly bandaged then the wet plaster is applied. Sometimes, once the plaster is dry, the cast is split into two and the two halves are then re-bandaged on the outside. This allows for any swelling that may occur.

Open or compound fractures – these have to be thoroughly cleansed in the operating room to remove debris prior to being set because a broken bone exposed to the open air is at increased risk of infection.

Long bones – long bones, like the bone of the thigh *(femur)*, are difficult to keep aligned and, in adults, are generally treated by internal nailing. Children may need traction for a couple of days prior to setting in a cast. Once the two ends of bone start to show signs of healing, the leg and hip joint should be immobilized in plaster of Paris. In other cases, pins are inserted above and below the fracture and secured to an external frame or 'fixator' under a general anesthetic.

EYES, EARS, NOSE AND THROAT INJURIES

Management of injuries of the eyes, ears, nose, and throat focuses on airway management and initial stabilization of the injury. Bilateral comparisons can assist in identifying injuries and changes.

EYE INJURIES

Foreign Objects

If a foreign object is present locate the object and attempt to remove object with the edge of a sterile dressing or rubber-tipped tweezers while avoiding the application of pressure to the object, causing the object to retreat further into the eye. Do not attempt to remove the foreign object if embedded in the lid or globe. If unable to remove the object place dressing over the eye and advise the patient to limit eye movement.

Injured Globes

If the orbit is injured treat any open wounds using Soft Tissue Injury Guidelines previously reviewed. If the eyeball is injured treat all open wounds and protect the eye using a cone or cup over the insured eye with bulky sterile dressings positioned to prevent the application of pressure. Do not apply pressure.

Impaled Object

Impaled Objects should not be removed, but should be immobilized by securing the object using a cone or cup over the impaled object with bulky sterile dressings positioned to stabilize the eye and prevent eye movement.

Avulsed Eye

Do not attempt to put the eye back in its socket and cover the eye with moist and sterile saline soaked dressings. Secure the eye using a cone or cup over the avulsed eye and bulky sterile dressings positioned to stabilize the eye and prevent eye movement.

Burns *(Corneal Abrasions)*

Treat as per burn guidelines and apply moist, sterile and saline soaked dressings loosely over the eye*(s)*.

Chemical Burns

Treat as per burns guidelines and avoid contaminating parts of the patient, including patient's other eye and orifices. Remove any contact lenses if present and use water to thoroughly flush the eyes, while refraining from the use of chemical antidotes or neutralizing agents. Irrigate under the eyelids and direct the stream of water away from the uninjured eye.

EAR INJURIES

Soft Tissue

Soft tissue injures should follow established guidelines and injuries should be handled gently, as there is often considerable pain accompanying ear injuries.

Fluid & Blood Discharge

Do not use direct pressure while applying bulky sterile dressings, assess patient for possible skull fracture and treat for shock if appropriate.

Foreign Object

Do not attempt to remove the object when medical personnel is available, and when the wound in non-life-threatening. With difficult visualization, it is likely the object has been embedded in the ear tissue, or may not be easily accessible. Avoid pressing the object further into the ear cavity and place bulky dressing over the ear.

Impaled Object

Do not remove the object when medical personnel will soon be available. However, immobilize and secure the object using bulky sterile dressings positioned to stabilize said object, preventing further movement.

Avulsed Ear

Locate and save avulsed parts and treat using standard Soft Tissue Injury guidelines.

NASAL INJURIES

Nosebleeds

Establish ABC's *(Airway, Breathing, Circulation),* control bleeding and apply cold packs to the nose, while making preparations and precautions for vomiting to likely occur. Do not allow patient to blow nose and position the patient upright and learning forward, while cautioning the patient to avoid swallowing and to spit out any blood.

Nose bleeds could indicate head injury so avoid pinching the nostrils and in cases associated with head injury in an unconscious patient, maintenance of the airway is the first priority. Section may be required to keep the airway clear and dressings should be placed below the nostrils to control further bleeding.

Foreign Object

Do not attempt to remove embedded objects while establishing ABC's. Control bleeding when present by applying dressings below the nostrils and applying cold packs to the nose *(if required).*

Throat Injury

Maintain a high level of suspicion for cervical spine injury while continuously monitoring the patient for a compromised airway due to swelling. Ensure any direct pressure applied to control hemorrhaging does not compromise the airway. If external bleeding from the neck cannot be controlled with direct pressure control the bleeding by using the carotid pressure point. Pressure should not be applied to both carotid arteries at the same time.

Burn Treatment

Establish ABC's and consider inhalation injury with potential airway compromise if any of the following clinical indicators are present;

I. History of altered mental status
II. History of confinement in a burning environment
III. Singed eyebrows and/or nasal hair
IV. Carbon deposits in orifices
V. Acute inflammatory changes in the oropharynx *(area around the uvula)*
VI. Carbonaceous sputum *(Burns to the nose, mouth and face)*
VII. Explosion with burns to head or torso

Presence of these findings suggests acute inhalation injury requiring immediate care and close monitoring for changes in the patients respiratory status, immediate medical help should is required. Burn treatment requires you to remove all jewelry, and external objects that have not been effused. Do not apply ointment to burns and do not pop/rupture blisters. Cold compresses should not be used for paint control, but cool saline or water should be applied to the burns until the burning process has stopped. Maintain high concentration of oxygen delivery. Do not allow your patient to walk.

In closing

This guide focuses on injuries that are most likely to happen when the SHTF and can be treated, injuries that require surgical help and assistance were not explained for obvious reasons. However, you can continue to read more advanced procedures.

BUSH SURVIVAL

HOW TO START A FIRE

Fire has several uses. Everyone should know how to start one, even though it is an essential survival skill, most do not know how to start a fire. Fire will provide warmth, water sanitation, and food preparation in addition to a means of defense.

Friction based fire making is not for the faint of heart. It's probably the most difficult of all the non-match based methods. There are different techniques you can use to make a fire with friction, but the most important aspect is the type of wood you use for the fire board and spindle.

HAND DRILL FIRE

I. Build a tinder nest. Your tinder nest will be used to create the flame you get from the spark you're about to create. Make a tinder nest out of anything that catches fire easily, like dry grass, leaves, and bark.

II. Make your notch. Cut a v-shaped notch into your fire board and make a small depression adjacent to it.

III. Place bark underneath the notch. The wood will be used to catch an ember from the friction between the spindle and fireboard.

IV. Start spinning. Place the spindle into the depression on your fire board. Your spindle should be about 2 feet long for this to work properly. Maintain pressure on the board and start rolling the spindle between your hands, running them quickly down the spindle. Keep doing this until an ember is formed on the board.

FIRE PLOUGH

I. Prepare your fireboard. Cut a groove in the fireboard. This will be your track for the spindle.
II. Rub vigorously and take the tip of your spindle and place it in the groove of your fireboard. Start rubbing the tip of the spindle up and down the groove.
III. Start the fire by having your tinder nest at the end of the fireboard, so that you'll plow embers into as you're rubbing. Once you catch one, blow the nest gently and get that fire going.

FLINT BASED FIRE

I. It's always a good idea to carry around a good flint and steel set with you on a camping trip.
II. If you're caught without a flint and steel set, you can always improvise by using quartzite and the steel blade of your pocket knife. You most likely do not have any char, so a piece of fungus or birch will do.
III. Grip the rock and birch/fungus. Take hold of the piece of rock between your thumb and forefinger. Make sure an edge is hanging off a couple inches. Grasp the char between your thumb and the flint.
IV. Strike the flint hard. Grab the back of the steel striker or use the back of your blade. Strike the steel against the flint several times. Sparks from the steel will fly off and land on birch/fungus.
V. Start the fire by folding your birch/fungus into the tinder nest and gently blow on it to start a flame.

BATTERY / STEEL WOOL FIRE

I. Stretch out the Steel Wool. You want it to be around 6 inches wide.

II. Rub the battery on the steel wool. Hold the steel wool in one hand and the battery in the other. Any battery will do. Rub the side of the battery with the contacts on the wool. The wool will begin to burn. Gently blow on it to create the fire.

III. Transfer the burning wool to your tinder nest. The wool's flame will go out quickly, so don't waste any time.

BUILD A LEAN TO

Access whether or not your situation requires shelter by gauging the weather and any other human based factors. Search for a healthy tree that has a low sturdy branch that is approximately six feet above the ground.

Gather materials to build your shelter. The materials needed for a shelter include; branches, small pine branches and leaves, relatively dry branches that are easy to remove. Avoid using excessively dried out materials for safety reasons.

Build the walls by leaning the longer branches against both sides of the sturdy branch of your tree, thus forming a tent structure. Place one branch after the other, tightly placed in order by pushing the bottom of the branch into the ground.

Place the pine branches and miscellaneous foliage on the outside of your Lean To. Then, place larger branches on top of the foliage to create a relatively sealed roof.

After everything is in place you can use paracord or vines to fasten the tops of the branches to one another. This is not necessary but will offer better protection during poor weather conditions.

When possible, improvise on this design by elevating your bed a foot off the ground to avoid unsavory animals poking around. Pad your bed with loose foliage and etc.

CHEAT SHEETS

Whistling

Whistling will carry approximately 1 to 2 miles, sometimes further in the wilderness, while your voice or shouting will only carry a few hundred yards. You will also be able to signal for much longer periods of time in intervals of three high-pitched blasts.

Fire

During darkness fire is the most effective visual signal for help; it also does pretty well during the day. You can build three fires to from a triangle, which is the international signal for help. As soon as your time and situation permit, build a signal. Do not light your signal with scarce resources unless you have a specific target you're signaling.

Smoke

During Daylight, you can build a smoky fire by using dense brush, using the smoke to attract attention. The international distress signal for help would be three columns of smoke. You can use a thick blanket (do not allow the fabric to make contact with open fires) to create your signals. By smothering your fire with green leaves, moss, water and etc. the fire will produce an attractive white smoke. Rubber, oil-soaked rags, and other polymer based scrap will create dark smoke. The color of your smoke must contrast with the skyline to be clearly seen for miles.

Signal Mirror

A commonly used and basic signaling device is a small mirror used to reflect the sun in a specific direction. During times of high visibility the flashes from a mirror can be seen for up to ten miles, and with practice you could possibly achieve a range of fifty miles.

Ground to Air Signals

Using your surroundings; rocks, logs, foliage and etc., create symbols that are at least nine to eighteen feet long, for larger signals use to same ratio. Keep in mind, signals should contrast with the ground to be easily seen and placed in an open area that can be spotted from the air.

Symbol	Meaning
V	Require Assistance
X	Require Medical Assistance
N	No or Negative Response
Y	Yes or Affirmative
↑	Proceed in this direction
SOS	Extreme Distress

Morse code

Morse code is widely known throughout many American institutions such as; the armed forces, boy scouts, HAM radio operators and etc. When PERSEC *(Personal Security)* or situational awareness requires the use of basic coded communication, Morse code should be used.

Morse code guidelines

I. A dash is equal to three dots.
II. The space between parts of the same letter is equal to one dot.
III. The space between two letters is equal to three dots.
IV. The space between two words is equal to seven dots.

A	•—	U	••—
B	—•••	V	•••—
C	—•—•	W	•——
D	—••	X	—••—
E	•	Y	—•——
F	••—•	Z	——••
G	——•		

H	••••		
I	••		
J	•———		
K	—•—	1	•————
L	•—••	2	••———
M	——	3	•••——
N	—•	4	••••—
O	———	5	•••••
P	•——•	6	—••••
Q	——•—	7	——•••
R	•—•	8	———••
S	•••	9	————•
T	—	0	—————

MULTILINGUAL EMERGENCY TRANSLATIONS

One of the most common trends seen in emergency situations is the shortcomings of Americans' ability to communicate effectively. A simple misunderstanding due to language barriers could lead to hostile situations. You can use this cheat sheet to communicate with other survivors that are not fluent in English.

SPANISH EMERGENCY PHRASES

I have an emergency. → ***"Yo tengo una emergencia."***

I am here to help. → ***"Estoy aquí para ayudar a."***

I need food. → ***"Necesito comida."***

I need water. → ***"Necesito agua."***

Please send help immediately. → ***"Por favor envie ayuda immediatamente."***

My name is _______________. → ***"Me lllamo ____________."***

I am armed. → ***"Yo estoy armado."***

Stay away! Keep your distance. → ***"No acercarse!"***

Get down on the ground. → ***"Bajar en el suelo."***

FRENCH EMERGENCY PHRASES

I have an emergency. → ***"J'ai une urgence."***

I am here to help. → ***"Je suis ici pour aider."***

I need food. → ***"J'ai besoin de nourriture."***

I need water. → ***"J'ai besoin d'eau."***

Please send help immediately. → ***"Veuillez envoyer l'aide immédiatement."***

My name is ______________. → ***"Mon nom est ___________."***

I am armed. → ***"Je suis armé."***

Stay away! Keep your distance. → ***"Gardez votre distance!"***

Get down on the ground. → ***"Obtenez vers le bas au sol."***

ITALIAN EMERGENCY PHRASES

I have an emergency. → ***"Ho un'emergenza."***

I am here to help. → ***"Io sono qui per aiutare."***

I need food. → ***"Ho bisogno di cibo."***

I need water. → ***"Ho bisogno di acqua."***

Please send help immediately. → ***"Si prega di inviare immediatamente aiuto."***

My name is ______________. → ***"Il mio nome è ___________."***

I am armed. → ***"Ci sono armati."***

Stay away! Keep your distance. → ***"Mantenere le distanze!"***

Get down on the ground. → ***"Scendere a terra."***

RUSSIAN EMERGENCY PHRASES

I have an emergency. → ***"Ich habe einen Notfall."***

I am here to help. → ***"Ich bin hier zu helfen."***

I need food. → ***"Ich benötige Nahrung."***

I need water. → ***"Ich benötige Wasser."***

Please send help immediately. → ***"Senden Sie bitte Hilfe sofort."***

My name is ______________. → ***"Mein Name ist ___________."***

USCROW

I am armed. → ***"Wir sind bewaffnet."***

Stay away! Keep your distance. → ***"Halten Sie Ihren Abstand!"***

Get down on the ground. → ***"Erhalten Sie unten aus den Grund."***

Tech Frequencies

Band	***Frequencies (In MHz)***	***Notes***
80 Meters	3.525 - 3.600 CW	200-watt limit
40 Meters	7.025 - 7.125 CW	200-watt limit
15 Meters	21.025 - 21.200	CW 200-watt limit
10 Meters	28.100 - 28.300	CW, RTTY, Data 200-watt limit
	28.300 - 28.500	CW, Phone, Image 200-watt limit

General Frequencies

Band	Frequency	Mode
160/60/30 Meters	All	
80 Meters	3.525-3.600	CW, RTTY, Data
	3.800-4.000	CW, Phone, Image
40 Meters	7.025-7.125	CW, RTTY, Data
	7.175-7.300	CW, Phone, Image
20 Meters	14.025-14.150	CW, RTTY, Data
	14.225-14.350	CW, Phone, Image
15 Meters	21.025-21.200	CW, RTTY, Data
	21.275-21.450	CW, Phone, Image
17/12/10 Meters	All	
Above 50 MHz	All	

Q Signals

QRL	Is the frequency busy? The frequency is busy. Please do not interfere.
QRM	Abbreviation for interference from other signals.
QRN	Abbreviation for interference from natural or man-made static.
QRO	Shall I increase power? Increase power.
QRP	Shall I decrease power? Decrease power.
QRQ	Shall I send faster? Send faster (WPM).
QRS	Shall I send more slowly? Send more slowly (_WPM).
QRT	Shall I stop sending? Stop sending.
QRU	Have you anything more for me? I have nothing more for you.
QRV	Are you ready? I am ready.
QRX	Standby.
QRZ	Who is calling me?
QSB	Abbreviation for signal fading.
QSL	Received and understood.
QSO	Abbreviation for a contact.
QST	General call preceding a message addressed to all amateurs.
QSX	I am listening on __ kHz.
QSY	Change to transmission on another frequency (or to __ kHz).
QTH	What is your location? My location is ___.

Channel Spacing and Offsets

HAM radio repeater stations retransmit other stations' signals. Repeaters are helpful in finding emergency broadcasting messages.

Band	Output	Offset
6 Meters	51.62-51.98	-500 KHz
	52.5-52.98	
	53.5-53.98	
2 Meters	145.2-145.5	-600 KHz
	146.61-147.00	-600 KHz
	147.00-147.39	+600 KHz
220 MHz	223.85-224.98	-1.6 MHz
440 MHz	442-445	+5 MHz
	447-450	-5 MHz
1296 MHz	1282-1288	-12 MHz

www.ingramcontent.com/pod-product-compliance
Lightning Source LLC
Chambersburg PA
CBHW070356290526
45790CB00004B/1510
* 9 7 8 1 4 8 2 7 8 3 5 2 0 *